CHAUCER FOR CHILDREN

KNIGHT SQUIRE BOY WIFE OF BATH PRIORESS CHAUCER (A CLERK) FRIAR MINE HOST
MONK SUMMONER PARDONER SECOND NUN FRANKLIN

MINE HOST ASSEMBLING THE CANTERBURY PILGRIMS

CHAUCER FOR CHILDREN

A Golden Key

By Mrs. H. R. Haweis

ILLUSTRATED WITH EIGHT COLOURED PICTURES AND
NUMEROUS WOODCUTS BY THE AUTHOR

'Doth now your devoir, yonge knightes proude!'

YESTERDAY'S CLASSICS

ITHACA, NEW YORK

Cover and arrangement © 2023 Yesterday's Classics, LLC.

This edition, first published in 2023 by Yesterday's Classics, an imprint of Yesterday's Classics, LLC, is an unabridged republication of the text originally published by Chatto & Windus, London in 1882. For the complete listing of the books that are published by Yesterday's Classics, please visit www.yesterdaysclassics.com. Yesterday's Classics is the publishing arm of Gateway to the Classics which presents the complete text of hundreds of classic books for children at www.gatewaytotheclassics.com.

ISBN: 978-1-63334-233-0

Yesterday's Classics, LLC
PO Box 339
Ithaca, NY 14851

CHIEFLY FOR THE USE AND PLEASURE OF

MY LITTLE LIONEL,

FOR WHOM I FELT THE NEED OF SOME BOOK OF THE KIND,

I HAVE ARRANGED AND ILLUSTRATED THIS

CHAUCER STORY-BOOK.

CONTENTS

FOREWORDS TO THE SECOND EDITION ix

FOREWORDS xi

CHAUCER THE TALE-TELLER 1

CANTERBURY TALES:—

    Chaucer's Pilgrims..................... 17

    Chaucer's Prologue.................... 18

    The Knight's Tale 34

    The Friar's Tale 57

    The Clerk's Tale 65

    The Franklin's Tale 84

    The Pardoner's Tale................... 92

MINOR POEMS:—

    Complaint of Chaucer to his Purse 100

    Two Rondeaux 101

    Virelai............................... 102

    Good Counsel of Chaucer............. 104

NOTES ON THE PICTURES 107

LIST OF ILLUSTRATIONS

COLOURED PICTURES

	PAGE		PAGE
I. PILGRIMS STARTING	Frontispiece	V. GRISELDA'S MARRIAGE	69
II. DINNER IN THE OLDEN TIME	2	VI. GRISELDA'S BEREAVEMENT	72
III. LADY CROSSING THE STREET	6	VII. DORIGEN AND AURELIUS	86
IV. FAIR EMELYE	37	VIII. THE RIOTER	97

WOODCUTS

	PAGE		PAGE
I. TOURNAMENT	Title-page	XVI. THE FRIAR	25
II. TABLE	2	XVII. THE MERCHANT	26
III. HEAD-DRESSES	2	XVIII. THE CLERK	27
IV. CHAUCER'S PORTRAIT	3	XIX. THE SERJEANT-OF-LAW	28
V. MAPS OF OLD AND MODERN LONDON	4	XX. THE FRANKLIN	28
VI. LADIES' HEAD-DRESSES	5	XXI. TABLE DORMANT	28
VII. SHOE	6	XXII. THE DOCTOR OF PHYSIC	29
VIII. JOHN OF GAUNT	7	XXIII. THE WIFE OF BATH	29
IX. SHIP	8	XXIV. THE PARSON	30
X. STYLUS	10	XXV. THE PLOUGHMAN	30
XI. THE KNIGHT	19	XXVI. THE SUMMONER	31
XII. THE SQUIRE	20	XXVII. THE PARDONER	31
XIII. THE YEOMAN	21	XXVIII. MINE HOST	32
XIV. THE PRIORESS	22	XXIX. KNIGHTS IN ARMOUR	48
XV. THE MONK	24	XXX. KNIGHTS IN ARMOUR	48

FOREWORDS TO THE SECOND EDITION

IN revising *Chaucer for Children* for a New Edition, I have fully availed myself of the help and counsel of my numerous reviewers and correspondents, without weighting the book, which is really designed for children, with a number of new facts, and theories springing from the new facts, such as I have incorporated in my Book for older readers, *Chaucer for Schools*.

Curious discoveries are still being made, and will continue to be, thanks to the labours of men like Mr. F. J. Furnivall, and many other able and industrious scholars, encouraged by the steadily increasing public interest in Chaucer.

I must express my sincere thanks and gratification for the reception this book has met with from the press generally, and from many eminent critics in particular; and last, not least, from those to whom I devoted my pleasant toil, the children of England.

M. E. HAWEIS.

FOREWORDS.

To the Mother

A CHAUCER for Children may seem to some an impossible story-book, but it is one which I have been encouraged to put together by noticing how quickly my own little boy learned and understood fragments of early English poetry. I believe that if they had the chance, many other children would do the same.

I think that much of the construction and pronunciation of old English which seems stiff and obscure to grown up people, appears easy to children, whose crude language is in many ways its counterpart.

The narrative in early English poetry is almost always very simply and clearly expressed, with the same kind of repetition of facts and names which, as every mother knows, is what children most require in story-telling. The emphasis * which the final E gives to many words is another thing which helps to impress the sentences on the memory, the sense being often shorter than the sound.

It seems but natural that every English child should know something of one who left so deep an impression on his age, and on the English tongue, that he has been called by Occleve "the finder of our fair language." For in his day there was actually no *national* language, no *national* literature, English consisting of so many dialects, each having its own literature intelligible to comparatively few; and the Court and educated classes still adhering greatly to Norman-French for both speaking and writing. Chaucer, who wrote for the people, chose the best form of English, which was that spoken at Court, at a time when English was regaining supremacy over French; and the form he adopted laid the foundation of our present National Tongue.

---

* I use the word 'emphasis' in the same sense as one might speak of a *crotchet* in music, to which you count two, being more emphatic than a quaver, to which you count one.

Chaucer is, moreover, a thoroughly religious poet, all his merriest stories having a fair moral; even those which are too coarse for modern taste are rather *naïve* than injurious; and his pages breathe a genuine faith in God, and a passionate sense of the beauty and harmony of the divine work. The selections I have made are some of the most beautiful portions of Chaucer's most beautiful tales.

I believe that some knowledge of, or at least interest in, the domestic life and manners of the 13th, 14th, and 15th centuries, would materially help young children in their reading of English history. The political life would often be interpreted by the domestic life, and much of that time which to a child's mind forms the *dryest* portion of history, because so unknown, would then stand out as it really was, glorious and fascinating in its vigour and vivacity, its enthusiasm, and love of beauty and bravery. There is no clearer or safer exponent of the life of the 14th century, as far as he describes it, than Geoffrey Chaucer.

As to the difficulties of understanding Chaucer, they have been greatly overstated. An occasional reference to a glossary is all that is requisite; and, with a little attention to a very simple general rule, anybody with moderate intelligence and an ear for musical rhythm can enjoy the lines.

In the first place, it must be borne in mind that the *E* at the end of the old English words was usually a syllable, and must be sounded, as *Aprillē, swootĕ*, &c.

Note, then, that Chaucer is always *rhythmical*. Hardly ever is his rhythm a shade wrong, and therefore, roughly speaking, *if you pronounce the words so as to preserve the rhythm* all will be well. When the final *e* must be sounded in order to make the rhythm right, sound it, but where it is not needed leave it mute. *

Thus:—in the opening lines—

<u>Glossary</u>.

when, showers, sweet	Whan that | *April* | *le* with | his *schowr* | *es* swoote
pierced, root	The drought | of Marche | hath per | cèd to | the roote
such, liquor	And bath | ud eve | ry veyne | in swich | licour
flower	Of whiche | vertue | engen | drèd is | the flour. (*Prologue*.)

You see that in those words which I have put in italics the final E must be sounded slightly, for the rhythm's sake.

small birds make	And *sma* | *le fow* | *les* ma | ken me | lodie
sleep, all	That sle | pen al | the night | with o | pen yhe. (*Prologue*.)

---

* Those who wish to study systematically the grammar, and construction of the metre, I can only refer to the best authorities, Dr. R. Morris and Mr. Skeat, respectively. It would be superfluous to enter on these matters in the present volume.

Again, to quote at random—

<small>GLOSSARY.</small>

lark, messenger	The bu | sy *lark* | *e* mess | ager | of day,	
saluteth, her, morning	Salu | eth in | hire song | the *mor* | *we* gray.	*(Knight's Tale.)*
legs, lean	Ful *long* | *e* wern | his leg | gus, and | ful lene;	
	Al like | a staff | ther was | no calf | y-sene.	*(Prologue—'Reve.')*

or in Chaucer's exquisite greeting of the daisy—

always	Knelyng | alwey | til it | unclo | sèd was	
small, soft, sweet	Upon | the *sma* | *le, sof* | *te, swo* | *te* gras.	*(Legend of Good Women.)*

How much of the beauty and natural swing of Chaucer's poetry is lost by translation into modern English, is but too clear when that beauty is once perceived; but I thought some modernization of the old lines would help the child to catch the sense of the original more readily: for my own rendering, I can only make the apology that when I commenced my work I did not know it would be impossible to procure suitable modernized versions by eminent poets. Finding that unattainable, I merely endeavoured to render the old version in modern English as closely as was compatible with sense, and the simplicity needful for a child's mind; and I do not in any degree pretend to have rendered it in poetry.

The beauty of such passages as the death of Arcite is too delicate and evanescent to bear rough handling. But I may here quote some of the lines as an example of the importance of the final *e* in emphasizing certain words with an almost solemn music.

speech, fail	And with | that word | his *spech* | *e fail* | *e* gan;	
	For fro | his feete | up to | his brest | was come	
overtaken	The cold | of deth | that hadde | him o | ver nome;	
now, arms	And yet | moreo | ver in | his *ar* | *mes* twoo	
gone	The vi | tal strength | is lost, | and al | agoo.	
without	Only | the in | tellect, | withou | ten more,	
heart, sick	That dwel | led in | his *her* | *te* sik | and sore,	
began to fail, felt death	Gan *fayl* | *e* when | the *her* | *te felt* | *e* deth.	*(Knight's Tale.)*

There is hardly anything finer than Chaucer's version of the story of these passionate young men, up to the touching close of Arcite's accident and the beautiful patience of death. In life nothing would have reconciled the almost animal fury of the rivals, but at the last such a resignation comes to Arcite that he gives up Emelye to Palamon with a sublime effort of self-sacrifice. Throughout the whole of the Knight's Tale sounds as of rich organ music seem to peal from the page; throughout the Clerk's

Tale one seems to hear strains of infinite sadness echoing the strange outrages imposed on patient Grizel. But without attention to the rhythm half the grace and music is lost, and therefore it is all-important that the child be properly taught to preserve it.

I have adhered generally to Morris's text (1866), being both good and popular, * only checking it by his Clarendon Press edition, and by Tyrwhitt, Skeat, Bell, &c., when I conceive force is gained, and I have added a running glossary of such words as are not immediately clear, on a level with the line, to disperse any lingering difficulty.

In the pictures I have been careful to preserve the right costumes, colours, and surroundings, for which I have resorted to the MSS. of the time, knowing that a child's mind, unaided by the eye, fails to realize half of what comes through the ear. Children may be encouraged to verify these costumes in the figures upon many tombs and stalls, &c., in old churches, and in old pictures.

In conclusion I must offer my sincere and hearty thanks to many friends for their advice, assistance, and encouragement during my work; amongst them, Mr. A. J. Ellis, Mr. F. J. Furnivall, and Mr. Calderon.

Whatever may be the shortcomings of the book, I cannot but hope that many little ones, while listening to Chaucer's Tales, will soon begin to be interested in the picturesque life of the middle ages, and may thus be led to study and appreciate 'The English Homer' † by the pages I have written for my own little boy.

ACCENT OF CHAUCER.

THE mother should read to the child a fragment of Chaucer with the correct pronunciation of his day, of which we give an example below, inadequate, of course, but sufficient for the present purpose. The whole subject is fully investigated in the three first parts of the treatise on 'Early English Pronunciation, with special reference to Shakespere and Chaucer,' by Alexander J. Ellis, F.R.S.

The *a* is, as in the above languages, pronounced as in *âne*, *appeler*, &c. *E* commonly, as in *écarté*, &c. The final *e* was probably indistinct, as in German now, *habe*, *werde*, &c.—not unlike the *a* in *China*: it was lost before a vowel. The final *e* is still sounded by the French in singing. In old French verse, one finds it as indispensable to the rhythm as in Chaucer,—and as graceful,—hence probably the modern retention of the letter as a syllable in vocal music.

---

* "No better MS. of the 'Canterbury Tales' could be found than the Harleian MS. 7334, which is far more uniform and accurate than any other I have examined; it has therefore been selected, and faithfully adhered to throughout, as the text of the present edition. Many clerical errors and corrupt readings have been corrected by collating it, line for line, with the Lansdowne MS. 851, which, notwithstanding its provincial peculiarities, contains many excellent readings, some of which have been adopted in preference to the Harleian MS." (Preface to Morris's Revised Ed. 1866.) This method I have followed when I have ventured to change a word or sentence, in which case I have, I believe, invariably given my authority.

† Roger Ascham.

Ou is sounded as the French *ou*.

I generally as on the Continent, *ee*: never as we sound it at present.

Ch as in Scotch and German.

I quote the opening lines of the Prologue as the nearest to hand.

Whan that Aprille with his schowres swoote	Whan that Aprilla with his shōōrĕs sohta
The drought of Marche hath perced to the roote,	The drŏŏkht of March hath pairsed to the rohta,
And bathud every veyne in swich licour,	And bahthed ev'ry vīn in sweech licōōr,
Of which vertue engendred is the flour;	Of which vairtú enjendrèd is the flōōr;
Whan Zephirus eek with his swete breethe	Whan Zephirŏŏs aik with his swaita braitha
Enspirud hath in every holte and heethe	Enspeered hath in ev'ry holt and haitha
The tendre croppes, and the yonge sonne	The tendra croppes, and the yŏŏnga sŏŏnna
Hath in the Ram his halfe cours i-ronne,	Hath in the Ram his halfa cōōrs i-rŏŏnna,
And smale fowles maken melodie,	And smahla fōōles mahken melodee-a,
That slepen al the night with open yhe,	That slaipen al the nikht with ohpen ee-a,
So priketh hem nature in here corages—&c.	So pricketh hem nahtúr in heer coràhges, &c.

It will thus be seen that many of Chaucer's lines end with a *dissyllable*, instead of a single syllable. *Sote, rote, brethe, hethe,* &c. (having the final *e*), are words of two syllables; *corages* is a word of three, *àges* rhyming with *pilgrimages* in the next line. It will also be apparent that some lines are lengthened with a syllable too much for strict *metre*—a licence allowed by the best poets,—which, avoiding as it does any possible approach to a doggrel sound, has a lifting, billowy rhythm, and, in fact, takes the place of a 'turn' in music. A few instances will suffice:—

'And though that I no wepne have in this place.'

'Have here my troth, tomorwe I nyl not fayle,
Withouten wityng of eny other wight.'

'As any raven fether it schon for-blak.'

'A man mot ben a fool other yong or olde.'

I think that any one reading these lines twice over as I have roughly indicated, will find the accent one not difficult to practise; and the perfect rhythm and ring of the lines facilitates matters, as the ear can frequently guide the pronunciation. The lines can scarcely be read too slowly or majestically.

I must not here be understood to imply that difficulties in reading and accentuating Chaucer are chimerical, but only that it is possible to understand and enjoy him without as much difficulty as is commonly supposed. In perusing the whole of Chaucer, there must needs be exceptional readings and accentuation, which in detail only a student of the subject would comprehend or care for.

The rough rule suggested in the preface is a good one, as far as the rhythm goes: as regards the sound, I have given a rough example.

I will quote a fragment again from the Prologue as a second instance:—

Ther was also a nonne, a prioresse,	Ther was ahlsoa a nŏŏn, a preeoressa,
That of hire smylyng was ful symple and coy;	That of her smeeling was fŏŏl sim-pland cooy;
Hire gretteste ooth nas but by Seynte Loy;	Heer graitest ohth nas bŏŏt bee Sī-ent Looy,
And sche was cleped Madame Eglentyne.	And shay was cleppèd Màdam Eglanteena.
Ful wel sche sang the servise devyne,	Fŏŏl well shay sang the *servicĕ divinä*,
Entuned in hire nose ful semyly;	Entúned in heer nohsa fŏŏl saimaly;
And Frensch sche spak ful faire and fetysly,	And French shai spahk fŏŏl fēr and faitisly,
Aftur the scole of Stratford atte Bowe,	Ahfter the scohl of Strahtford ahtta Bow-a,
For Frensch of Parys was to hire unknowe.	For French of Pahrees was toh her ŏŏn-know-a.

Observe *simpland* for *simple and:* simple being pronounced like a word of one syllable. With the common English pronunciation the lines would not scan. 'Vernicle,' 'Christofre,' 'wimple,' 'chilindre,' 'companable,' &c., are further instances of this mute *e*, and may be read as French words.

CHAUCER THE TALE-TELLER

I.

DO you like hearing stories? I am going to tell you of some one who lived a very long time ago, and who was a very wise and good man, and who told more wonderful stories than I shall be able to tell *you* in this little book. But you shall hear some of them, if you will try and understand them, though they are written in a sort of English different from what you are accustomed to speak.

But, in order that you really may understand the stories, I must first tell you something about the man who made them; and also why his language was not the same as yours, although it was English. His name was Chaucer—Geoffrey Chaucer. You must remember his name, for he was so great a man that he has been called the 'Father of English Poetry'—that is, the beginner or inventor of all the poetry that belongs to our England; and when you are grown up, you will often hear of Chaucer and his works.

II.

Chaucer lived in England 500 years ago—a longer time than such a little boy as you can even think of. It is now the year 1876, you know. Well, Chaucer was born about 1340, in the reign of King Edward III. We should quite have forgotten all Chaucer's stories in such a great space of time if he had not written them down in a book. But, happily, he did write them down; and so we can read them just as if he had only told them yesterday.

If you could suddenly spring back into the time when Chaucer lived, what a funny world you would find! Everybody was dressed differently then from what people are now, and lived in quite a different way; and you might think they were very uncomfortable, but they were very happy, because they were accustomed to it all.

People had no carpets in those days in their rooms. Very few people were rich enough to have glass windows. There was no paper on the walls, and very seldom any pictures; and as for spring sofas and arm-chairs, they were unknown. The seats were only benches placed against the wall: sometimes a chair was brought on grand occasions to do honour to a visitor; but it was a rare luxury.

The rooms of most people in those days had blank walls of stone or brick and plaster, painted white or coloured, and here and there—behind the place of honour, perhaps—hung a sort of curtain, like a large picture, made of needlework, called tapestry. You may have seen tapestry hanging in rooms, with men and women and animals worked upon it. That was almost the only covering for walls in Chaucer's time. Now we have a great many other ornaments on them, besides tapestry.

The rooms Chaucer lived in were probably like every one's else. They had bare walls, with a piece of tapestry hung here and there on them—a bare floor, strewn with rushes, which must have looked more like a stable than a sitting-room. But the rushes were better than nothing. They kept the feet warm, as our carpets do, though they were very untidy, and not always very clean.

When Chaucer wanted his dinner or breakfast, he did not go to a big table like that you are used to: the table came to him. A couple of trestles or stands were brought to him, and a board laid across them,  and over the board a cloth, and on the cloth were placed all the curious dishes they ate then. There was no such thing as coffee or tea. People had meat, and beer, and wine for breakfast, and dinner, and supper, all alike. They helped themselves from the common dish, and ate with their fingers, as dinner-knives and forks were not invented, and it was thought a sign of special good breeding to have clean hands and nails. Plates there were none. But large flat cakes of bread were used instead; and when the meat was eaten off them, they were given to the poor—for, being full of the gravy that had soaked into them, they were too valuable to throw away. When they had finished eating, the servants came and lifted up the board, and carried it off.

III.

And now for Chaucer himself! How funny you would think he looked, if you could see him sitting in his house! He wore a hood, of a dark colour, with a long tail to it, which in-doors hung down his back, and out of doors was twisted round his head to keep the hood on firm. This tail was called a liripipe.

He did not wear a coat and trousers like your father's, but a sort of gown, called a tunic, or dalmatic, which in one picture of him is grey and loose, with large sleeves, and bright red stockings and black boots; but on great occasions he wore a close-fitting tunic, with a splendid belt and buckle, a dagger, and jewelled garters, and, perhaps, a gold circlet round his hair. How much prettier to wear such bright colours instead of black! men and women dressed in green, and red, and yellow then; and when they walked in the streets, they looked as people look in pictures.

DINNER IN THE OLDEN TIME

GEOFFREY CHAUCER.

You may see how good and clever Chaucer was by his face; such a wise, thoughtful, pleasant face! He looks very kind, I think, as if he would never say anything harsh or bitter; but sometimes he made fun of people in a merry way. Words of his own, late in life, show that he was rather fat, his face small and fair. In manner he seemed 'elvish,' or shy, with a habit of staring on the ground, 'as if he would find a hair.'

All day he worked hard, and his spare time was given to 'studying and reading alway,' till his head ached and his look became dazed. *(House of Fame.)*

Chaucer lived, like you, in London. Whether he was born there is not known;* but as his father, John Chaucer, was a vintner in Thames Street, London, it is probable that he was. Not much is known about his parents or family, except that his grandfather, Richard Chaucer, was also a vintner; and his mother had an uncle who was a moneyer; so that he came of respectable and well-to-do people, though not noble. † Whether he was educated at Oxford or Cambridge, whether he studied for the bar or for the Church, there is no record to show; but there is no doubt that his education was a good one, and that he worked very hard at his books and tasks, otherwise he could not have grown to be the learned and cultivated man he was. We know that he possessed considerable knowledge of the classics, divinity, philosophy, astronomy, as much as was then known of chemistry, and, indeed, most of the sciences. French and Latin he knew as a matter of course, for the better classes used these tongues more than English—Latin for writing, and French for writing and speaking; for, by his translations from the French, he earned, early in life, a 'balade' of compliment from Eustache Deschamps, with the refrain, *'Grant translateur, noble Geoffroi Chaucier.'* It is probable, too, that he knew Italian, for, in his later life, we can see how he has been inspired by the great Italian writers, Dante, Petrarch, and Boccaccio.

It has recently been discovered that for a time (certainly in 1357) Geoffrey Chaucer, being then seventeen, was a page ‡ in the household of Elizabeth, Countess of Ulster, wife of Lionel, second son of King Edward III.; a position which he could not have held if he had not been a well-born, or at least well-educated, person. A page in those days was very different from what we call a page now—therefore we infer that the Chaucer family had interest at Court; for without that, Geoffrey could never have entered the royal service.

Most gentlemen's sons were educated by becoming pages. They entered the service of noble ladies, who paid them, or sometimes were even paid for receiving them. Thus young men learned courtesy of manners, and all the accomplishments of indoor and outdoor life—riding, the use of arms, &c.—and were very much what an *aide-de-camp* in the army now is. Chaucer, you see, held a post which many a nobly-born lad must have coveted.

There is a doubtful tradition that Chaucer was intended for a lawyer, and was a member of the Middle Temple (a large building in London, where a great many lawyers live still), and here, as they say, he was once fined two shillings for beating a Franciscan friar in Fleet Street.

If this be true, it must have been rather a severe beating; for two shillings was a far larger sum than it is now—equal to about sixteen shillings of our money. Chaucer was sometimes angry with

---

* Mr. Furnivall, among some of his recent interesting researches anent Chaucer, has discovered with certainty his father's name and profession.

† The position of Chaucer, and his wife, in the King's service, and that of the latter in the service of Constance, Duchess of Lancaster, shared with two ladies of rank, be well as their lifelong interest at Court, prove, I think, that neither of them was of mean parentage, and that they occupied a very good social *status*.

‡ See also p. 19, note §.

the friars at later times in life, and deals them some hard hits in his writings with a relish possibly founded on personal experience of some disagreeable friar.

At any rate, Chaucer never got fond of the friars, and thought they were often bad and mischievous men, who did not always *act* up to what they *said*. This is called *hypocrisy*, and is so evil a thing that Chaucer was quite right to be angry with people who were hypocrites.

IV.

Fleet Street still exists, though it was much less crowded with people in Chaucer's day than now. Indeed, the whole of London was very different from our London; and, oh, so much prettier! The streets within the London wall were probably thickly populated, and not over-healthy; but outside the wall, streets such as Fleet Street were more like the streets of some of our suburbs, or rather some foreign towns—the houses irregular, with curious pointed roofs, here and there divided by little gardens, and even green fields. I dare say, when Chaucer walked in the streets, the birds sang over his head, and the hawthorn and primrose bloomed where now the black smoke and dust would soon kill most green things. Thames Street was where Chaucer long lived in London, but, at one time in his life at least, it is certain that he occupied a tenement at Aldgate, which formed part of an old prison; and it is probable that at another he lived in the beautiful Savoy Palace with John of Gaunt, whilst his wife was maid of honour. In 1393, Chaucer was living at Greenwich, near which he had work in 1390—poor and asking his friend Scogan to intercede for him "where it would fructify;" and at the end of his life he had a house in Westminster, said to be nearly on the same spot on which Henry VII.'s Chapel now stands, and close to the Abbey where he is buried.

In those days it was the fashion, when the month of May* arrived, for everybody, rich and poor, to get up very early in the morning, to gather boughs of hawthorn and laurel, to deck all the doorways in the street, as a joyful welcoming of the sweet spring time. Chaucer alludes more than once to this beautiful custom. The streets must have been full of fragrance then. He also tells us how he loved to rise up at dawn in the morning, and go into the fresh green fields, to see the daisies open. You have often seen the daisies shut up at night, but I don't suppose you ever saw them opening in the morning; and I am afraid, however early you got up in London, you could not reach the fields quick enough to see that. But you may guess from this how much nearer the country was to the town 500 years ago. There were so many fewer houses built then, that within a walk you could get right into the meadows. You may see that by comparing the two maps I have made for you.

London was also much quieter. There were no railways—such things had never been heard of. There were not even any cabs or carriages. Sometimes a market cart might roll by, but not very often, and then everybody would run out to see what the unaccustomed clatter was all about. People had to walk everywhere, unless they were rich enough to ride on horseback, or lived near the river. In that case, they used to go in barges or boats on the Thames, as far as they could; for, strange as it may seem, even the King had no coach then.

I am afraid Geoffrey Chaucer would not recognize that 'dere and swete citye of London' in the great, smoky, noisy, bustling metropolis we are accustomed to, and I am quite sure he would not recognize the language; and presently I will explain what I meant by saying that though Chaucer spoke and wrote

---

* It must not be forgotten, in reading praises of warm and sunny May, often now a bleak and chilly month, that the seasons were a fortnight later at that time, May-day coming therefore in the middle of the month, and May ending in the middle of June. The change in the almanac was made in Italy in 1582, in England in 1752.

London in the 15th Century.

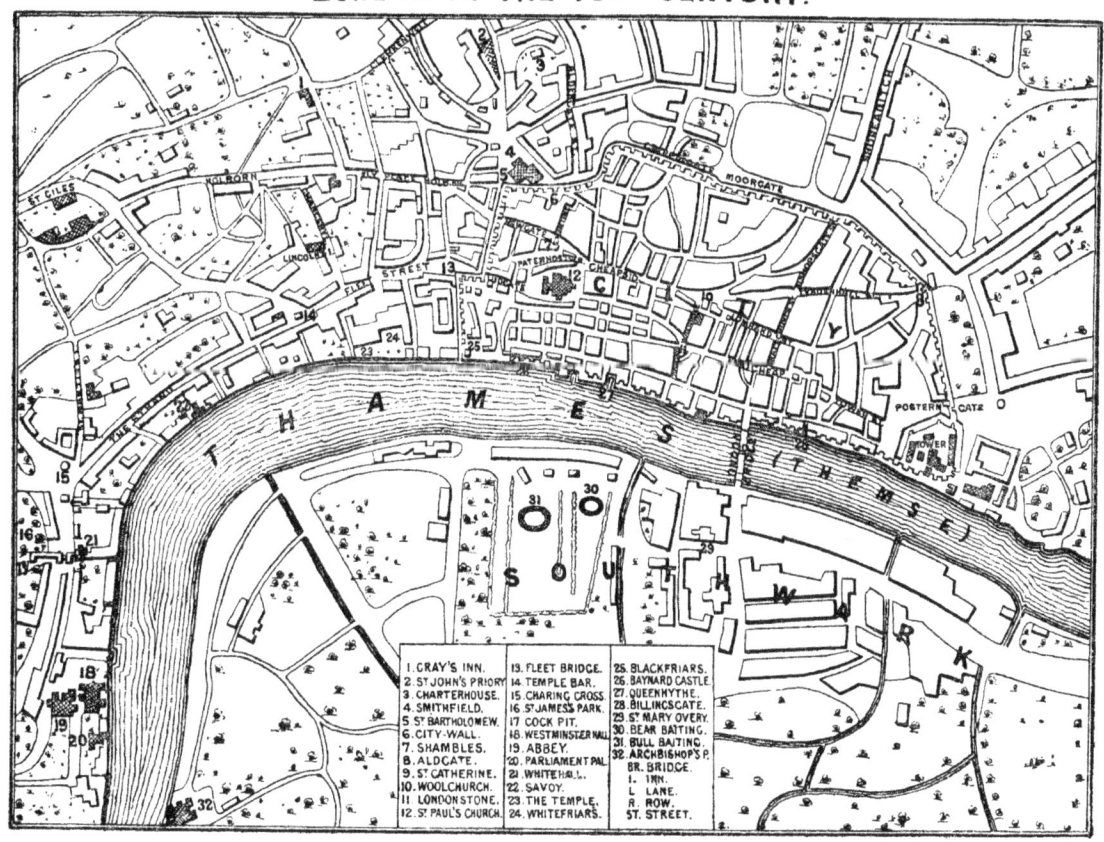

London in the 19th Century.

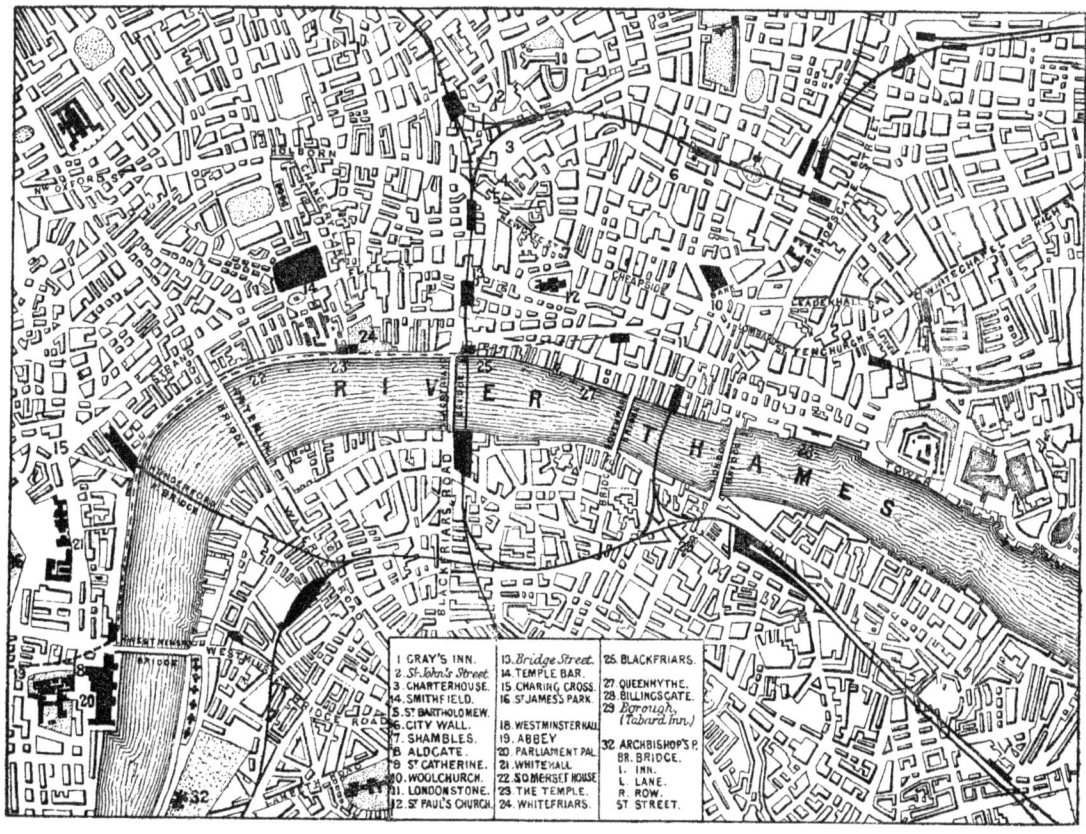

English, it was quite different from what we speak now. You will see, as you go on, how queerly all the words are spelt, so much so that I have had to put a second version side by side with Chaucer's lines, which you will understand more readily; and when I read them to you, you will see how different is the sound. These words were all pronounced slowly, almost with a drawl, while we nowadays have got to talk so fast, that no one who lived then would follow what we say without great difficulty.

V.

Chaucer's connection with the Court makes it probable that he lived during the greater part of his life in London; and it is pleasant to think that this great poet was valued and beloved in his day by the highest powers in the land. He held, at various times, posts in the King's household, which brought him more or less money, such as valet of the King's chamber, the King's esquire, &c.; and he found a fast friend in John of Gaunt, one of the sons of King Edward III.

In 1359 Chaucer became a soldier, and served in the army under this King, in an attack upon France, and was taken prisoner. It is supposed he was detained there about a year; and, being ransomed by Edward, when he came back to England, he married a lady named Philippa. She was probably the younger daughter of Sir Paon de Roet, of Hainault, * who came over to England in the retinue of Queen Philippa, who was also of Hainault. These two Philippas, coming from the same place, remained friends during all the Queen's life; for when Chaucer married Philippa de Roet, she was one of the Queen's maids of honour; and, after her marriage, the Queen gave her an annual pension of ten marks † (£50), which was continued to her by the King after Queen Philippa died. Some people say Chaucer's wife was also the Queen's god-daughter. ‡

If you would like to know what Chaucer's wife looked like, I will tell you. I do not know what she was like in the face, but I can tell you the fashion of the garb she wore. I like to believe she had long yellow hair, which Chaucer describes so often and so prettily. Chaucer's wife wore one of those funny head-dresses like crowns, or rather like boxes, over a gold net, with her hair braided in a tress, hanging down her back. She had a close green § dress, with tight sleeves, reaching right down over the hand, to protect it from the sun and wind; and a

---

* Dr. Morris writes—"The old supposition that the Philippa whom Chaucer married was the daughter of Sir Paon de Roet (a native of Hainault and King of Arms of Guienne), and sister to Katherine, widow of Sir Hugh Swynford, successively governess, mistress, and wife of John of Gaunt, Duke of Lancaster, was founded on heraldic grounds. The Roet arms were adopted by Thomas Chaucer. Then Thomas Chaucer was made (without the slightest evidence) Geoffrey's son, and Philippa Roet was then made Geoffrey's wife." And again, "It is possible that Philippa Chaucer was a relative or namesake of Geoffrey, and that he married her in the spring or early summer of 1374." It is, however, much less likely that there were so many Chaucers about the Court, unconnected with each other, than that the common supposition is correct. At any rate, *until there is any evidence to the contrary*, this tradition may be fairly accepted. The recent discovery, in the Record Office, of Thomas Chaucer's deed, by Mr. Hunter, sealed with a seal bearing the legend, 'S Ghofrai Chaucer,' seems to support the tradition.

† A mark was 13*s*. 4*d*. of our money, but the buying power of money was eight or ten times greater than at present. So that, although ten marks was only £6 12*s*. of our currency, it was fully equal to £50.

‡ There are entries mentioning Philippa Chaucer in 1366, 1372, and 1374. The former names her as one of the ladies of the bedchamber to Queen Philippa, who conferred the annuity of ten marks in September, 1366. In 1372 John of Gaunt conferred on Philippa Chaucer an annuity of £10 (equal to £100). Her name is mentioned when the grant to Chaucer of a pitcher of wine daily is commuted into money payment, June 13, 1374, by John of Gaunt (again a pension of £10), for good services rendered by the Chaucers to the said Duke, his consort, and his mother the Queen.

§ Green was the favourite colour of the time.

very long skirt, falling in folds about her feet, sometimes edged with beautiful white fur, ermine, or a rich grey fur, called vair. The colour of this grey fur was much liked, and when people had light grey eyes, of somewhat the same colour, it was thought very beautiful. Many songs describe pretty ladies with 'eyes of vair.'

When noble persons went to Court, they wore dresses far more splendid than any to be seen now—dresses of all colours, worked in with flowers and branches of gold, sometimes with heraldic devices and strange figures, and perfectly smothered in jewels. No one has pearls, and emeralds, and diamonds sewn on their gowns now; but in the fourteenth century, rich people had the seams of their clothes often covered with gems. The ladies wore close-fitting dresses, with splendid belts, or *seints*, round their hips, all jewelled; and strings of glittering jewels hung round their necks, and down from the belt, and on the head-dress. People did not wear short sleeves then, but long ones, made sometimes very curiously with streamers hanging from the elbow; a long thin gauze veil, shining with silver and gold; and narrow pointed shoes, much longer than their feet, which, they thought, made the foot look slender. If ladies had not had such long shoes, they would never have showed beneath their long embroidered skirts, and  they would always have been stumbling when they walked. It was a very graceful and elegant costume that Chaucer's wife wore; but the laws of England probably forbade her to wear silk, which was reserved for nobles. When she walked out of doors, she had tall clogs to save her pretty shoes from the mud of the rough streets; and when she rode on horseback with the Queen, or her husband Chaucer, she sat on a pillion, and placed her feet on a narrow board called a *planchette*. Many women rode astride, like the "Wife of Bath" whom Chaucer speaks of.

Now, perhaps, you would like to know whether Chaucer had any little children. We do not know much about Chaucer's children. We know he had a little son called Lewis, because Chaucer wrote a treatise for him when he was ten years old, to teach him how to use an instrument he had given him, called an *astrolabe*. * Chaucer must have been very fond of Lewis, since he took so much trouble for him, and he speaks to him very kindly and lovingly.

As Chaucer was married before 1366, it is likely that he had other children; and some people say he had an elder son, named Thomas, and a daughter Elizabeth. †

John of Gaunt, who was Chaucer's patron as I told you, was very kind to Thomas Chaucer, and gave him several posts in the King's household, as he grew up to be a man. And John of Gaunt heard that Elizabeth Chaucer wished to be a nun; and, in 1381, we find that he paid a large sum of money for her *noviciate* (that is, for her to learn to be a nun) in the Abbey of Barking.

A nun is a person who does not care for the amusements and pleasures which other people care for—playing, and dancing, and seeing sights and many people; but who prefers to go and live in a house called a nunnery, where she will see hardly any one, and think of nothing but being good, and helping the poor. And, if people think they can be good best in that way, they ought to become

---

* *Astrolabe:* a machine used at sea to measure the distances of stars. The quadrant now in use has superseded the astrolabe.

† Thomas Chaucer was born in or about 1367, and died in 1434. Elizabeth Chaucer's noviciate was paid for by John of Gaunt in 1381. If Elizabeth Chaucer was about 16 in 1381 she would have been born about 1365; and, therefore, as far as dates are concerned, either Thomas or Elizabeth may well have been elder children of the poet: the chances being that he married in 1361-64. Moreover, John of Gaunt's interest in both of these persons, Thomas Chaucer and Elizabeth Chaucer, gives this a colour of probability. At the same time Chaucer seems to have been no uncommon name.

Chaucer's exceptional notice of his little son Lewis who must have been born in 1381, the year of Elizabeth's novitiate, since Chaucer describes him as being ten years old in his treatise on the astrolabe in 1391, may have been due to the appearance of a 'Benjamin' rather late in life.

A LADY CROSSING THE STREET IN THE OLDEN TIME

nuns. But I think people can be just as good living at home with their friends, without shutting themselves in a nunnery.

Now I must leave off telling you about Chaucer's wife and children, and go on to Chaucer himself.

VI.

Chaucer was, as I told you, the friend of one of the sons of the King, Edward III. Not the eldest son, who was, as you know, Edward the Black Prince, the great warrior, nor Lionel, the third son, whom he had served when a boy, but the fourth son, John of Gaunt, who had a great deal of power with the King.

John of Gaunt was the same age as Chaucer.

When John of Gaunt was only 19 (the year that Chaucer went with the army to France), he married a lady called Blanche of Lancaster, and there were famous joustings and great festivities of every kind. In this year, it has been supposed, Chaucer wrote a poem, 'The Parliament of Birds,' to celebrate the wedding. Another long poem, called 'The Court of Love,' is said to have been written by him about this time—at any rate, in very early life.

John of Gaunt

When Chaucer came back to England, and got married himself, he was still more constantly at Court, and there are many instances recorded of John's attachment to both Chaucer and Philippa all his life. Among others we may notice his gifts to Philippa of certain 'silver-gilt cups with covers,' on the 1st of January in 1380, 1381, and 1382.

It is touching to see how faithful these two friends were to each other, and how long their friendship lasted. The first we hear of it was about 1359, the year when John married Blanche, and for forty years it remained unbroken. Nay, it grew closer and closer, for in 1394, when John of Gaunt and Chaucer were both middle-aged men, John married Philippa's sister (Sir Paon Roet's elder daughter), so that Chaucer became John of Gaunt's brother. *

When John of Gaunt was in power he never forgot Chaucer. When he became unpopular it was Chaucer's turn to be faithful to him; and faithful he was, whatever he suffered, and he did suffer for it severely, and became quite poor at times, as you will see. Directly John came into power again up went Chaucer too, and his circumstances improved. There are few friendships so long and so faithful on both sides as this was. †

VII.

Chaucer was employed by Edward III. for many years as envoy, which is a very important office. It can only be given to a very wise and shrewd man. This proves the great ability of Chaucer in other things besides making songs and telling stories. He had to go abroad, to France, Italy, and elsewhere, on the King's private missions; and the King gave him money for his services, and promoted him to great honour.

---

* On the hypothesis, of course, that Chaucer married a Roet.

† For many new and curious facts about Chaucer, see my *Chaucer for Schools*, "Chaucer's Court Life and Position."

Petrarch, a great Italian poet and patriot, whose name you must not forget. Petrarch was then living at Arqua, two miles from Padua, a beautiful town in Italy; and though Petrarch was a much older man than Chaucer—more than twenty years older—it seems only natural that these two great men should have tried to see each other; for they had much in common. Both were far-famed poets, and both, in a measure, representatives of the politics, poetry, and culture of their respective countries.

Still, some people think they could never have met, because the journey from Florence to Padua was a most difficult one. Travelling was hard work, and sometimes dangerous, guides being always necessary: you could not get a carriage at any price, for carriages were not invented. In some places there was no means of going direct from city to city at all—not even on horseback—there being actually no roads. So that people had to go on foot or not at all. If they went, there were rocks and rivers to cross, which often delayed travellers a long time.

Chaucer, as the King's envoy, must have had attendants, even for safety's sake, with him, and much luggage, and that would of course make travelling more difficult and expensive. He most likely went a great part of the way by sea, in a vessel coasting along the Mediterranean to Genoa and Leghorn, and so by Pisa to Florence: you may trace his route in a map. Doubtless, he had neither the means nor the will to go all the way to Padua on his own account. So you see people hold different opinions about this journey, and no one can be quite sure whether Chaucer did see Petrarch or not.

In 1373 Chaucer wrote his 'Life of St. Cecile;' and about that time, perhaps earlier, the 'Complaint to Pity.'

VIII.

I am not going to tell you everything that the King and John of Gaunt did for Chaucer. You would get tired of hearing about it. I will only say that Chaucer was 'holden in greate credyt,' and probably had a real influence in England; for, connected as he was with John of Gaunt, I dare say he gave him advice and counsel, and John showed the King how shrewd and trustworthy Chaucer was, and persuaded him to give him benefits and money.

John's wife, Blanche of Lancaster, died in 1369, and so did his mother, Queen Philippa. Chaucer wrote a poem called 'The Death of Blanche the Duchess,' in honour of this dead Blanche. John married another wife in the next year, and got still more powerful, and was called King of Castile, in Spain, because his new wife was the daughter of a King of Castile. But all this made no difference in his affection for Chaucer. He always did what he could for Chaucer.

I will give you some instances of this.

Soon after Chaucer's return from his journey to Florence, he received a grant of 'a pitcher of wine' every day 'from the hands of the King's butler.' This seems like a mark of personal friendship more than formal royal bounty; but it was worth a good deal of money a year. Less than two months afterwards he received, through John of Gaunt's goodwill, a place under Government called 'Comptrollership of the Customs' of the Port of London. This was a very important post, and required much care, shrewdness, and vigilance; and the King made it a condition that all the accounts of his office were to be entered in Chaucer's own handwriting—which means, of course, that Chaucer was to be always present, seeing everything done himself, and never leaving the work to be done by anybody else, except when sent abroad by the King's own royal command. Only three days after this, John of Gaunt himself made Chaucer a grant of £10 a year for life, in reward for all the good service rendered by 'nostre bien ame Geffray Chaucer,' and 'nostre bien ame Philippa sa femme,' to himself, his duchess, and to his mother, Queen Philippa, who was dead. This sum of money does not sound much; but it was a great deal in those days, and was fully equal to £100 now.

The very next year the King gave Chaucer the 'custody' of a rich ward (a ward is a person protected or maintained by another while under age), named Edmond Staplegate, of Kent; and when this ward married, Chaucer received a large sum of money (£104 = £1,040). *

Then Chaucer's care in the Customs' office detected a dishonest man, who tried to ship wool abroad without paying the lawful duty; this man was fined for his dishonesty, and the money, £71 4s. 6d., was made a present to Chaucer—a sum equal to £700.

So you see it seemed as if John of Gaunt could never do enough for him; because all these things, if not done by John himself, were probably due to his influence with the King.

IX.

The Black Prince died about that time, and Edward III. did not long survive him. He died in 1377. Then the Black Prince's little son, Richard, who was only eleven years old, became King of England; but as he was too young to reign over the country, his three uncles governed for him. These three uncles were John of Gaunt, Duke of Lancaster; the Duke of York; and the Duke of Gloucester.

And all this time Chaucer was very well looked after, you may be sure, for John of Gaunt was then more powerful than the King. Chaucer was still Comptroller of the Customs; and, before long, John gave him a second post of a similar kind, called 'Comptroller of the Petty Customs.'

But all this good luck was not to go on for ever. The people were not so fond of John of Gaunt as Chaucer was, because, in governing them, he was very ambitious and severe. They got angry with everything he did, and with everybody who remained his friend. So, of course, they did not like Chaucer.

This was a very troublous time. The Crown (represented by the King's uncles) wanted one thing, and the great barons wanted another, and the people or lower classes wanted another! These were called the three great opposing parties, and each wanted to have all the power. At last some of the barons sided with the King's party, and others sided with the people; so there were then two opposing parties quarrelling and hating each other. John of Gaunt would have liked to be King himself; but the people were unhappy, and very discontented with his government, and he began to have much less power in the kingdom.

---

* In these cases, the sum received on the marriage of the ward was legally a fine on the marriage.

The people knew that John of Gaunt was obliged to go with an army into Portugal, and they began to make plans to get their own way when his back was turned. When he was gone, they said that John of Gaunt did not govern them well, and had given government posts to men who did not do their duty, and neglected their work, and Chaucer was one of them.

Then there was what was called a 'Commission of Inquiry' appointed, which means a body of men who were free to examine and reform everything they chose in the country. Their power was to last a whole year; and these men looked into all that Chaucer had done in the 'Customs' offices. They did not find anything wrong, as far as we know, but still they sent away Chaucer in disgrace, just as if they had. And this made him very poor. It was a harsh thing to do, and unjust, if they were not certain he had been neglecting his work; and John of Gaunt was out of the country, and could not help him now. This was in the year 1386.

A great deal has been said and written about this matter. Some people still believe that Chaucer really did neglect his duties, though the conditions that he should attend to everything himself had been so very strict; * that he had probably absented himself, and let things go wrong. But such people forget that these conditions were formally done away with in 1385, when Chaucer was finally released from personal drudgery at the Customs, and allowed to have a deputy, or person under him to do his work.

They forget, too, how Chaucer had plunged into political matters directly afterwards, at a time when party feeling was intensely strong, the people and John of Gaunt being violently opposed to each other; and how Chaucer took up the part of his friend warmly, and sat in the House of Commons as representative of Kent, one of the largest counties of England, on purpose to support the ministers who were on John of Gaunt's side. This alone would be enough to make the opposing party hate Chaucer, and this doubtless was the reason of their dismissing him from both his offices in the Customs as soon as ever they were able, to punish him for his attachment to the Duke of Lancaster's (John of Gaunt's) cause.

But Chaucer never wavered or changed. And his faithfulness to his friend deserves better than the unjust suspicion that his disgrace was warranted by neglect of his duties. Chaucer was too good, and too pious, and too honourable a man to commit any such act. He submitted to his disgrace and his poverty unmoved; and after the death of his wife Philippa, which happened in the following summer, nothing is known of him for several years, except that he was in such distress that he was actually obliged to part with his two pensions for a sum of money in order to pay his debts.

During all the eventful years that followed Edward III.'s death, up to this time, Chaucer had been writing busily, in the midst of his weightier affairs. The 'Complaint of Mars,' 'Boece,' 'Troilus and Cressida,' the 'House of Fame,' and the 'Legend of Good Women,' all of which I hope you will read some day, were written in this period; also some reproachful words to his scrivener, who seems to have written out his poems for him very carelessly. Some persons think that Chaucer's pathetic 'Good Counsel,' and his short 'Balade sent to King Richard,' reflect the disappointment and sadness at his changed lot, which he must have felt; and that, therefore, these poems were written at about the same time.

---

* See Chambers's Encyclopædia, 'Chaucer'.

X.

In 1389 there was another great change in the government. The King, being of age, wished to govern the country without help, and he sent away one of his uncles, who was on the people's side, and asked John of Gaunt to come back to England. John of Gaunt's son was made one of the new ministers. Immediately Chaucer was thought of. He was at once appointed Clerk of the King's Works—an office of some importance—which he was permitted to hold by deputy; and his salary was two shillings per day—that is £36 10s. 0d. a-year, equal to about £370 of our money.

It seems that Chaucer kept this appointment only for two years. Why, we cannot tell. * While he held this office (viz., Sept. 1390) a misfortune befell him. Some notorious thieves attacked him, near the 'foule Ok' (foul Oak), and robbed him of £20 (nearly £200 present currency) of the King's money, his horse, and other movables. This was a mishap likely enough to overtake any traveller in those days of bad roads and lonely marshes, for there was no great protection by police or soldiery in ordinary cases. The King's writ, in which he forgives Chaucer this sum of £20, is still extant.

What he did, or how he lived, for some time after his retirement from the King's Works in 1391, is not known; but in 1394, King Richard granted him a pension of £20 (= £200 present currency) per annum for life. This was the year when John of Gaunt married Chaucer's sister-in-law; but, in spite of this rich alliance, I fear Chaucer was still in great distress, for we hear of many small loans which he obtained on this new pension during the next four years, which betray too clearly his difficulties. In 1398, the King granted him letters to protect him against arrest—that is, he wrote letters forbidding the people to whom Chaucer owed money to put him in prison, which they would otherwise have done.

It is sad that during these latter years of his life, the great poet who had done so much, and lived so comfortably, should have grown so poor and harassed. He ought to have been beyond the reach of want. He had had large sums of money; his wife's sister was Duchess of Lancaster; his son † was holding grants and offices under John of Gaunt. Perhaps he wasted his money. ‡ But we cannot know exactly how it all came about at this distance of time. And one thing shows clearly how much courage and patience Chaucer had; for it was when he was in such want in 1388, two years after he had been turned out of the Customs, that he was busiest with the greatest work of his life, called the Canterbury Tales. Some men would have been too sad after so much disgrace and trouble, to be able to write stories and verses; but I think Chaucer must have felt at peace in his mind—he must have known that he did not deserve all the ill-treatment he got—and had faith that God would bring him through unstained.

XI.

The Canterbury Tales are full of cheerfulness and fun; full of love for the beautiful world, and full of sympathy for all who are in trouble or misery. The beauty of Chaucer's character, and his

---

* See *Chaucer for Schools*, p.22, for further details.

† I have assumed that Thomas Chaucer was Geoffrey Chaucer's son, as there is no proof to the contrary, and a probability in point of dates that he was.

‡ See 'Notes by the Way,' p. 103.

deep piety, come out very clearly in these tales, as I think you will see. No one could have sung the 'ditties and songs glad' about birds in the medlar trees, and the soft rain on the 'small sweet grass,' and the 'lily on her stalk green,' and the sweet winds that blow over the country, whose mind was clouded by sordid thoughts, and narrow, selfish aims. No one could have sung so blithely of 'fresh Emily,' and with such good-humoured lenity even of the vulgar, chattering 'Wife of Bath,' whose heart was full of angry feelings towards his fellow-creatures. And no one, who was not in his heart a religious man, could have breathed the words of patience with which Arcite tries to comfort his friend, in their gloomy prison—or the greater patience of poor persecuted Griselda—or the fervent love of truth and honourable dealing, and a good life, which fills so many of his poems—or a hundred other touching prayers and tender words of warning. There was a large-heartedness and liberality about Chaucer's mind, as of one who had mixed cheerfully with all classes, and saw good in all. His tastes were with the noble ranks among whom he had lived; but he had deep sympathy with the poor and oppressed, and could feel kindly even to the coarse and the wicked. He hated none but hypocrites; and he was never tired of praising piety and virtue.

Chaucer wrote a great many short poems, which I have not told you of. Many have been lost or forgotten. Some may come back to us in the course of time and search. All we know of, you will read some day, with the rest of the CANTERBURY TALES not in this book: a few of these poems I have placed at the end of the volume; and among them one 'To his empty Purse,' written only the year before his death. *

There is only a little more I can tell you about Chaucer's life before we begin the stories. We got as far as 1398, when the King gave Chaucer letters of protection from his creditors.

About this time another grant of wine was bestowed on him, equal to about £4 a year, or £40 of our money. In the next year, King Richard, who had not gained the love of his subjects, nor tried to be a good King, was deposed—that is, the people were so angry with him that they said, "You shall not be our King any more;" and they shut him up in a tower, and made his cousin, Henry, King of England. Now this Henry was the son of John of Gaunt, by his first wife, Blanche, and had been very badly treated by his cousin, the King. He was a much better man than Richard, and the people loved him. John of Gaunt did not live to see his son King, for he died while Henry was abroad; and it must have been a real grief to Chaucer, then an old man of sixty,† when this long and faithful friend was taken from him.

Still it is pleasant to find that Henry of Lancaster shared his father's friendship for Chaucer. I dare say he had been rocked on Chaucer's knee when a little child, and had played with Chaucer's children. He came back from France, after John of Gaunt's death, and the people made him King, and sent King Richard to the castle of Pomfret (where I am sorry to say he was afterwards murdered).

The new King had not been on the throne four days before he helped Chaucer. John of Gaunt himself could not have done it quicker. He granted him an annuity of £26 13s. 4d. a year, in addition to the other £20 granted by Richard.

The royal bounty was only just in time, for poor old Chaucer did not long survive his old friend, the Duke of Lancaster. He died about a year after him, when Henry had been King thirteen months.

John of Gaunt was buried in St. Paul's, by the side of his first and best-loved wife, Blanche; Geoffrey Chaucer was buried in Westminster Abbey.

* See *Chaucer for Schools*.

† Remembering the discussion raised as to the year of Chaucer's birth, coupled with the tradition of his venerable looks, we may suggest that in those days men were older at sixty than now. The average duration of life was shorter, and the paucity of comforts probably told on appearance.

So ended the first, and almost the greatest, English writer, of whom no one has spoken an ill word, and who himself spoke no ill words.

Poet, soldier, statesman, and scholar, 'truly his better ne his pere, in school of my rules could I never find. . . . In goodness of gentle, manly speech he passeth all other makers.' *

XII.

And now for Chaucer's 'speech.' How shall I show you its 'goodness,' since it is so difficult to read this old English? Wait a bit. You will soon understand it all, if you take pains at the first beginning. Do not be afraid of the funny spelling, for you must remember that it is not so much that Chaucer spells differently from us, as that we have begun to spell differently from Chaucer. He would think our English quite as funny, and not half so pretty as his own; for the old English, when spoken, sounded very pretty and stately, and not so much like a 'gabble' as ours.

I told you a little while ago, you know, that our talking is much faster than talking was in Chaucer's time; it seems very curious that a language can be so changed in a few hundred years, without people really meaning to change it. But it has changed gradually. Little by little new words have come into use, and others have got 'old-fashioned.' Even the English of *one* hundred years ago was very unlike our own. But the English of *five* hundred years ago was, of course, still more unlike.

XIII.

Now, I have put, as I told you, two versions of Chaucer's poetry on the page, side by side. First, the lines as Chaucer made them, and then the same lines in English such as we speak. You can thus look at both, and compare them.

I will also read you the verses in the two ways of pronouncing them, Chaucer's way and our way: but when you have grown a little used to the old-fashioned English, you will soon see how much prettier and more musical it sounds than our modern tongue, and I think you will like it very much. Besides, it is nice to be able to see the words as Chaucer put them, so as to know exactly how he talked.

In Chaucer's time a great deal of French was spoken in England, and it was mixed up with English more than it is now. The sound of old French and old English were something the same, both spoken very slowly, with a kind of drawl, as much as to say—"I am in no hurry. I have all day before me, and if you want to hear what I have got to say, you must wait till I get my words out."

So if you wish to hear Chaucer's stories, you must let him tell them in his own way, and try and understand his funny, pretty language. And if you do not pronounce the words as he meant, you

* Author of the 'Testament of Love.'

will find the verses will sound quite ugly—some lines being longer than others, and some not even rhyming, and altogether in a jumble.

XIV.

Chaucer himself was very anxious that people should read his words properly, and says in his verses, as if he were speaking to a human being—

Glossary.

great diversity	And for there is so grete dyversité
tongue	In Englissh, * and in writynge of our tonge,
pray	So preye I God that non miswrité thee
defect	Ne thee mys-metere for defaute of tonge. (*Troilus.*)

To *mis-metre* is to read the *metre* wrong; and the metre is the length of the line. If you read the length all wrong, it sounds very ugly.

Now, suppose those lines were read in modern English, they would run thus:—

> And because there is so great a diversity
> In English, and in writing our tongue,
> So I pray God that none miswrite thee
> Nor mismetre thee through defect of tongue.

How broken and ragged it all sounds! like a gown that is all ragged and jagged, and doesn't fit. It sounds much better to read it properly.

You will find that when Chaucer's words are rightly pronounced, all his lines are of an even length and sound pretty. I don't think he ever fails in this. This is called having a musical ear. Chaucer had a musical ear. Some people who write poetry have not, and their poetry is good for nothing. They might as well try to play the piano without a musical ear; and a pretty mess they would make of that! †

XV.

When you find any very hard word in Chaucer's verses which you cannot understand, look in the glossary and the modern version beside them; and you will see what is the word for it nowadays. A few words which cannot be translated within the metre you will find at the bottom of the page; but think for yourself before you look. There is nothing like thinking for one's self. Many of the words are like French or German words: so if you have learnt these languages you will be able often to guess what the word means.

For instance, you know how, in French, when you wish to say, I *will not* go or I *am not* sure, two no's are used, *ne* and *pas:* Je *n'*irai *pas*, or je *ne* suis *pas* sûr. Well, in Chaucer's time two no's were used in English. He would have said, "I *n'*ill *nat* go," and "I *n'*am *nat* sure."

---

* Alluding to the numerous dialects in use in England at the time.

† The mother should here read to the child some lines with the proper pronunciation: see Preface, pp. x., xi.

There are many lines where you will see two no's. "I n'am nat precious." "I ne told no deintee." "I wol not leve no tales." "I ne owe hem not a word." "There n' is no more to tell," &c. Sometimes, however, *ne* is used by itself, without *not* or *nat* to follow. As "it n'is good," "I n'ill say—or sain," instead of "it is not good—I will not say."

And, as in this last word sain (which only means *say*), you will find often an *n* at the end of words, which makes it difficult to understand them; but you will soon cease to think that a very alarming difficulty if you keep looking at the modern version. As, "I shall nat *lien*" (this means *lie*). "I wol nat *gon*" (*go*): "*withouten* doubt" (*without*). "Ther wold I *don* hem no pleasance" (*do*); "thou shalt *ben* quit" (*be*). "I shall you *tellen*" (*tell*).

And I think you will also be able to see how much better some old words are for expressing the meaning, than our words. For instance, how much nicer 'flittermouse' is than 'bat.' That is an old North-country word, and very German (Fledermaus). When you see a little bat flying about, you know it is a bat because you have been told: but 'flitter-mouse' is better than bat, because it means 'floating mouse.' Now, a bat *is* like a mouse floating in the air. The word expresses the movement and the form of the creature.

Again—the old word 'herteles' (heartless), instead of without courage, how well it expresses the want of courage or spirit: we often say people have no heart for work, or no heart for singing, when they are sad, or ill, or weak. Heartless does not always mean cowardly; it means that the person is dejected, or tired, or out of spirits. We have left off using the word heartless in that sense, however, and we have no word to express it. When *we* say heartless, we mean cruel or unkind, which is a perfectly different meaning.

Again, we have no word now for a meeting-time or appointment, as good as the old word 'steven:' we use the French word '*rendezvous*' as a noun, which is not very wise. 'Steven' is a nice, short, and really English word which I should like to hear in use again.

One more instance. The word 'fret' was used for devouring. This just describes what we call 'nibbling' now. The moth fretting a garment—means the moth devouring or nibbling a garment.

This is a word we have lost sight of now in the sense of *eating*; we only use it for 'complain-ing' or 'pining.' But a *fretted* sky—and the *frets* on a guitar—are from the old Saxon verb *frete*, to eat or devour, and describe a wrinkly uneven surface, like the part of a garment fretted by the moth. So you must not be impatient with the old words, which are sometimes much better for their purpose than the words we use nowadays.

CANTERBURY TALES.

CHAUCER'S PILGRIMS.

SOME of Chaucer's best tales are not told by himself. They are put into the mouths of other people. In those days there were no newspapers—indeed there was not much news—so that when strangers who had little in common were thrown together, as they often were in inns, or in long journeys, they had few topics of conversation: and so they used to entertain each other by singing songs, or quite as often by telling their own adventures, or long stories such as Chaucer has written down and called the '*Canterbury Tales.*'

The reason he called them the '*Canterbury Tales*' was because they were supposed to be told by a number of travellers who met at an inn, and went together on a pilgrimage to a saint's shrine at Canterbury.

But I shall now let Chaucer tell you about his interesting company in his own way.

He begins with a beautiful description of the spring—the time usually chosen for long journeys, or for any new undertaking, in those days.

When you go out into the gardens or the fields, and see the fresh green of the hedges and the white May blossoms and the blue sky, think of Chaucer and his Canterbury Pilgrims!

Chaucer's Prologue.

GLOSSARY.

When, sweet	Whan that Aprille with his schowres swoote	When April hath his sweetest showers brought
root	The drought of Marche hath perced to the roote,	To pierce the heart of March and banish drought,
such liquor	And bathud every veyne in swich licour,	Then every vein is bathéd by his power,
flower	Of which vertue engendred is the flour;	With fruitful juice engendering the flower;
also, breath	Whan Zephirus * eek with his swete breeth	When the light zephyr, with its scented breath,
grove	Enspirud hath in every holte and heeth	Stirs to new life in every holt and heath
young	The tendre croppes, and the yonge sonne	The tender crops, what time the youthful sun
run	Hath in the Ram his halfe cours i-ronne,	Hath in the Ram his course but half-way run;
small birds make	And smale fowles maken melodie,	And when the little birds make melody,
sleep, eye	That slepen al the night with open yhe,	That sleep the whole night long with open eye,
pricketh them, their impulses	So priketh hem nature in here corages:—	So Nature rouses instinct into song,—
long, go	Thanne longen folk to gon on pilgrimages,	Then folk to go as pilgrims greatly long,
seek shores	And palmers † for to seeken straunge strondes,	And palmers hasten forth to foreign strands
distant saints	To ferne halwes, kouthe ‡ in sondry londes;	To worship far-off saints in sundry lands;
	And specially from every schires ende	And specially from every shire's end
go	Of Engelond, to Canturbury they wende,	Of England, unto Canterbury they wend,
blessed, seek	The holy blisful martir § for to seeke,	Before the blessed martyr there to kneel,
them sick	That hem hath holpen whan that they were seeke.	Who oft hath help'd them by his power to heal.

* *Zephyrus*, or Zephyr: the god of the west wind. It is become a name for the wind of summer.

† Pilgrims who have brought a palm branch from the Holy Land.

‡ *Kouthe:* past participle of the verb conne, to know, or to be able. It was used much as *savoir* is in French—to be able to do, to know how to do a thing. The verse means 'To serve the saints they could, or they knew of, or knew how to serve.'

§ Thomas Beket, Chancellor of Henry II. He was Archbishop of Canterbury for eight years, and was murdered by servants of the King in 1170. He was canonized, or made a saint, by the Pope, after his death, and pilgrimages were then constantly made to his tomb in Canterbury Cathedral. In those days it was usual in sickness or peril to vow a pilgrimage to the shrine of some saint who was supposed to be able to help people by interceding with God, when pilgrims prayed him to. Erasmus alludes to the quantities of offerings on Thomas Beket's shrine, given by those who believed the saint had healed or helped them.

It happened that one day in the spring, as I was resting at the Tabard * Inn, in Southwark, ready to go on my devout pilgrimage to Canterbury, there arrived towards night at the inn a large company of all sorts of people—nine-and-twenty of them: they had met by chance, all being pilgrims to Canterbury. † The chambers and the stables were roomy, and so every one found a place. And shortly, after sunset, I had made friends with them all, and soon became one of their party. We all agreed to rise up early, to pursue our journey together. ‡

But still, while I have time and space, I think I had better tell you who these people were, their condition and rank, which was which, and what they looked like. I will begin, then, with

The Knight.

GLOSSARY.

there, valuable } A KNIGHT § ther was and that a worthy man, / That from the tyme that he ferst bigan

A knight there was, and that a worthy man, / Who from the time in which he first began

* A tabard was an outer coat without sleeves, worn by various classes, but best known as the coat worn over the armour (see p. 48), whereon there were signs and figures embroidered by which to recognize a man in war or tournament: for the face was hidden by the helmet, and it was easier to detect a pattern in bright colours than engraved in dark steel. So, of course, the pattern represented the arms used by him. And thus the tabard got to be called the *coat of arms*. Old families still possess what they call their coat of arms, representing the device chosen by their ancestors in the lists; but they do not wear it any more: it is only a copy of the pattern on paper. A *crest* was also fastened to the helmet for the same purpose of recognition, and there is usually a 'crest' still surmounting the modern 'coat of arms.' The inn where Chaucer slept was simply named after the popular garment. It, or at least a very ancient inn on its site, was recently standing, and known as the Talbot Inn, High Street, Borough: Talbot being an evident corruption of Tabard. We may notice here, that the Ploughman, described later on, wears a tabard, which may have been a kind of blouse or smock-frock, but was probably similar in form to the knight's tabard.

† People were glad to travel in parties for purposes of safety, the roads were so bad and robbers so numerous.

‡ Probably all or many occupied but one bedroom, and they became acquainted on retiring to rest, at the ordinary time—sunset.

§ The word Knight (knecht) really means *servant*. The ancient knights attended on the higher nobles and were their *servants*, fighting under them in battle. For as there was no regular army, when a war broke out everybody who could bear arms engaged himself to fight under some king or lord, anywhere, abroad or in England, and was paid for his services. That was how hundreds of nobly born men got their living—the only way they could get it. This is what the knight Arviragus does in the 'Franklin's Tale;' leaving his bride, to win honour (and money) by fighting wherever he could.

The *squire* waited on the knight much as the knight did on the earl—much in the position of an aide-de-camp of the present day. The *page* served earl, knights, ladies. But knight, squire, and page were all honourable titles, and borne by noblemen's sons. The page was often quite a boy, and when he grew older changed his duties for those of squire, till he was permitted to enter the knighthood. The present knight is described as being in a lord's service, and fighting under him 'in his war,' but he was a man held in the highest honour.

20 — GOLDEN KEY TO CHAUCER

Glossary		
ride	To ryden out, he lovede chyvalrye,	To ride afield, loved well all chivalry,
frankness	Trouthe and honour, fredom and curtesie.	Honour and frankness, truth and courtesy.
war	Ful worthi was he in his lordes werre,	Most worthy was he in his master's war,
further	And therto hadde he riden, noman ferre,	And thereto had he ridden, none more far,
	As wel in Cristendom as in hethenesse,	As well in Christian as in heathen lands,
	And evere honoured for his worthinesse.	And borne with honour many high commands.

He had been at Alexandria when it was won: in Prussia he had gained great honours, and in many other lands. He had been in fifteen mortal battles, and had fought in the lists for our faith three times, and always slain his foe. He had served in Turkey and in the Great Sea. And he was always very well paid too. Yet, though so great a soldier, he was wise in council; and in manner he was gentle as a woman. Never did he use bad words in all his life, to any class of men: in fact

> He was a verray perfight, gentil knight.   He was a very perfect, noble knight.

As for his appearance, his horse was good, but not gay. He wore a gipon of fustian, all stained by his habergeon;* for he had only just arrived home from a long voyage.

The Squire.

there, son	With him ther was his sone, a yong SQUYER,	With him there was his son, a gay young squire,
merry	A lovyer, and a lusty bacheler,†	A bachelor and full of boyish fire,
locks curled	With lokkes crulle as they were layde in presse.	With locks all curl'd as though laid in a press,
guess	Of twenty yeer he was of age I gesse.	And about twenty years of age, I guess.
wonderfully nimble, great	Of his stature he was of evene lengthe, And wondurly delyver, and gret of strengthe.	In stature he was of an even length, And wonderfully nimble, and great of strength.

* See p. 48 and Appendix, p. 107.

† "On nommait *Bacheliers* les chevaliers pauvres, les *bas Chevaliers* . . . quand ceux-ci avaient reçu la chevalerie, on les appelait Chevaliers-Bacheliers . . . quant à l'Ecuyer (Squire) c'était le préntendant à la Chevalerie."—LEGRAND, *Fabliaux & Contes*.

Glossary		
had been	And he hadde ben somtyme in chivachie, *	And he had followed knightly deeds of war
	In Flaundres, in Artoys, and in Picardie,	In Picardy, in Flanders, and Artois,
little	And born him wel, as in so litel space,	And nobly borne himself in that brief space,
stand	In hope to stonden in his lady grace. †	In ardent hope to win his lady's grace.
	Embrowdid ‡ was he, as it were a mede	Embroidered was he, as a meadow bright,
	Al ful of fresshe floures, white and reede.	All full of freshest flowers, red and white;
playing on the flute	Syngynge he was, or flowtynge al the day;	Singing he was, or flute-playing all day,
	He was as fressh as is the moneth of May.	He was as fresh as is the month of May.
	Schort was his goune, with sleeves long and wyde.	Short was his gown, his sleeves were long and wide,
could, horse	Wel cowde he sitte on hors, and faire ryde.	Well he became his horse, and well could ride;
relate	He cowde songes wel make and endite,	He could make songs, and ballads, and recite,
also, draw pictures	Justne and eek daunce, and wel purtray and write.	Joust and make pretty pictures, dance, and write.

As for the young squire's manners—

	Curteys he was, lowly, and servysable,	Courteous he was, lowly, and serviceable,
carved	And carf § byforn his fadur at the table.	And carved before his father at the table.

The Yeoman.

no more	A YEMAN had he, and servantes nomoo	A yeoman had he (but no suite beside:
it pleased him	At that tyme, for him luste ryde soo;	Without attendants thus he chose to ride,)
	And he was clad in coote and hood of grene.	And he was clad in coat and hood of green.

* *Chivachie*: military expeditions.
† See page 45, note †.
‡ Mr. Bell considers that these two lines refer to the squire's complexion of red and white. Speght thinks it means freckled. But there is little doubt that the material of his dress is what Chaucer means, for there is no other instance of Chaucer calling a complexion *embroidered*, and gorgeously flowered fabrics embroidered with the needle were peculiar to the period and in common use.
§ As it was the custom for sons to do.

arrows	A shef of pocok arwes * bright and kene,	A sheaf of peacock-arrows bright and keen,
bore	Under his belte he bar ful thriftily,	Under his belt he carried thriftily;
arrow	Wel cowde he dresse his takel yomanly;	Well could he dress an arrow yeomanly!
arrows	His arwes drowpud nought with fetheres lowe,†	None of his arrows drooped with feathers low
bore	And in his hond he bar a mighty bowe.	And in his hand he held a mighty bow.
v. notes, p. 112.	A not-heed hadde he, with a broun visage.	A knot-head had he, and a sunburnt hue,
knew	Of woode-craft cowde he wel al the usage;	In woodcraft all the usages he knew;
bore	Upon his arme he bar a gay bracer,‡	Upon his arm a bracer gay he wore,
buckler	And by his side a swerd, and a bokeler,§	And by his side buckler and sword he bore,
	And on that other side a gay daggere,	While opposite a dagger dangled free;
dressed well	Harneysed wel, and scharp at poynt of spere;	Polished and smart, no spear could sharpe be.
ornament representing St. Christopher	A Cristofre on his brest of silver schene.	A silver 'Christopher' on his breast was seen,
	An horn he bar, the bawdrik‖ was of grene:	A horn he carried by a baldrick green:
forester, truly	A forster was he sothely, as I gesse.	He was a thorough forester, I guess.

The Prioress.

	Ther was also a Nonne, a PRIORESSE,	There also was a Nun, a Prioress,
her	That of hire smylyng was ful symple and coy;	Who of her smiling was most simple and coy;
oath	Hire grettest ooth¶ ne was but by seynt Loy,	Her greatest oath was only 'by St. Loy,'

* Peacocks' feathers on them instead of swans'.

† It was a sign of the yeoman's carefulness in his business that they stuck out from the shaft instead of drooping.

‡ *Bracer:* a leathern defence for the arm: a similar shield is now worn in archery.

§ *Bokeler*—buckler: a small shield—used chiefly for a warder to catch the blow of an adversary. Some pictures show the buckler to have been only the size of a plate, but it varied. In comparing the Wife of Bath's hat to a buckler, Chaucer could not have meant so small a one. It was usual for serving men of noble families to carry swords and bucklers when in attendance on them.

‖ *Bawdrik*—baldrick: ornamented strap to suspend the horn or dagger.

¶ Oaths were only too common among ladies as well as men. It was an exceptional refinement to use only a small oath. Tyrwhitt prints the name of the saint, Eloy, contraction of Eligius—a saint who, having been a worker in metals, was often invoked by smiths (see 'Friar's Tale'), &c.; but Dr. Morris says St. Loy is the old spelling of St. Louis of France, by whom the Prioress swore.

CHAUCER'S PROLOGUE

Glossary		
called	And sche was cleped madame Eglentyne.	And she was calléd Madame Eglantine.
	Ful wel sche sang the servíse devyne,	Full well she sang the services divine,
seemly	Entuned in hire nose * ful semyly,	Entunéd through her nose melodiously,
elegantly	And Frensch sche spak ful faire and fetysly,	And French she spoke fairly and fluently,
school	Aftur the scole of Stratford atte Bowe,	After the school of Stratford atte Bow,
her unknown	For Frensch of Parys was to hire unknowe.	For French of Paris—*that* she did not know.
meat, taught	At mete wel i-taught was sche withalle;	At meal-times she was very apt withal;
let	Sche leet no morsel from hire lippes falle,	No morsel from her lips did she let fall,
wetted	Ne wette hire fyngres in hire sauce deepe. †	Nor in her sauce did wet her fingers deep;
carry	Wel cowde sche carie a morsel, and wel keepe,	Well could she lift a titbit, and well keep,
fell	That no drope ne fil uppon hire breste.	That not a drop should fall upon her breast;
courtesy, pleasure	In curtesie was sett al hire leste.	To cultivate refinement was her taste.
	Hire overlippe wypude sche so clene, ‡	Her upper lip she ever wiped so clean
scrap	That in hire cuppe ther was no ferthing sene	That in her drinking-cup no scrap was seen
had drunk	Of grees, whan sche dronken hadde hire draught.	Of grease, when she had drank as she thought good.
seemly	Ful semely aftur hire mete sche raught.	And gracefully she reach'd forth for her food.
assuredly	And sikurly sche was of gret disport,	And she was very playful, certainly,
	And ful plesant, and amyable of port,	And pleasant, and most amiable to see.
ways	And peyned hire to counterfete cheere	And mighty pains she took to counterfeit
stately, manner	Of court, and ben estatlich of manere,	Court manners, and be stately and discreet,
worthy	And to ben holden digne of reverence.	And to be held as worthy reverence.
speak	But for to speken of hire conscience,	But then to tell you of her conscience!
	Sche was so charitable and so pitous §	She was so charitable and piteous
	Sche wolde weepe if that sche sawe a mous	That she would weep did she but see a mouse
	Caught in a trappe, if it were deed or bledde.	Caught in a trap, if it were dead or bled;
small hounds	Of smale houndes hadde sche, that sche fedde	And little dogs she had, which oft she fed
	With rostud fleissh, and mylk, and wastel breed. ‖	With roasted meat, and milk, and finest bread;
them	But sore wepte sche if oon of hem were deed,	But sore she wept if one of them were dead,

* Bell approves reading *voice* for nose, as Speght has actually done. It has not struck either of them that Chaucer is all the way through laughing at the fastidious and rather over-attractive nun!

† Knives and forks were not in use—people had to use their fingers; but some used them more agreeably than others.

‡ At meals one cup for drinking passed from guest to guest, instead of each having his own glass, as now. It was considered polite to wipe one's mouth well before drinking, so that the next drinker should find no grease in the wine. The great stress Chaucer lays on the pretty nun's courtesy seems to hint at very dirty habits among ordinary folk at meals!

§ Mr. Bell naïvely points out the innocence and 'ignorance of the ways of the world,' which pervade the whole of the 'simple Prioress's character;' but you will notice that in laughing at the cheerful nun's affectation of court manners, Chaucer never once gives her credit for very high or noble character, though he does not speak ill-naturedly. I have ere now alluded to his dislike of the Church, friars, nuns, and all included: and here he shows that her charitableness and compassion were spent on wholly inadequate objects. She is extravagant to the last degree in feeding her dogs, and weeping for dead mice; but nothing is said of charity to the poor, or any good works at all. She is too intent on fascinating everybody, and dressing smartly. There is sharp sarcasm in all this.

‖ *Wastel breed*—a kind of cake—the most expensive of all bread.

Glossary		
rod	Or if men smot it with a yerde smerte:	Or, haply, with a rod were smitten smart.
	And al was conscience and tendre herte.	And all was conscience and tender heart!
	Ful semely hire wymple * i-pynched was:	Most daintily her wimple plaited was:
well-proportioned, eyes, glass	Hire nose tretys: hire eyen grey as glas:	Her nose was straight; her eyes were grey as glass;
	Hire mouth ful smal, and therto softe and reed;	Her mouth was little, and so soft and red!
surely	But sikurly sche hadde a faire forheed.	Besides, she had a very fine forehead,
broad, think	It was almost a spanne brood, I trowe:	That measured nigh a span across, I trow!
certainly, undergrown	For hardily sche was not undurgrowe.	For certainly her stature was not low.
neat	Ful fetys was hire cloke, as I was waar.	And very dainty was the cloak she wore;
small	Of smal coral aboute hire arme sche baar	Around her arm a rosary she bore,
set of beads	A peire of bedes † gaudid al with grene;	Of coral small, with little gauds of green,
jewel, bright	And theron heng a broch of gold ful schene,	And thereon hung a golden locket sheen,
written	On which was first i-writen a crowned A,	On which was graven first a crownéd A,
	And after that, *Amor vincit omnia*.‡	And after, *Amor vincit omnia*.

The Prioress was attended by another nun, who acted as her chaplain, and three priests.

The Monk.

mastery	A MONK ther was, a fair for the maistrie,§	A monk there was—one sure to rise no doubt,
hunting	An out-rydere, that lovede venerye;	A hunter, and devoted rider out;
be	A manly man, to ben an abbot able.	Manly—to be an abbot fit and able,
dainty horse	Ful many a deynte hors hadde he in stable:	For many a dainty horse had he in stable;

* *Wimple:* a loose covering for the neck, close up to the chin, plaited daintily; worn especially by nuns.

† A rosary, the coral beads of which were divided by smaller ones, or gauds, of a green colour.

‡ 'Love conquers all things.' The Prioress might have twisted this device to refer to the text, 'The greatest of these is charity;' but the *double entendre* is apparent.

§ From a French phrase, *bone pur la maistrie*—good to excel all others. The monk bids fair to excel all others or outstrip the rest in promotion, on account of his worldliness.

CHAUCER'S PROLOGUE

GLOSSARY.

when, hear	And whan he rood, men might his bridel heere *	And when he rode, his bridle you could hear
jingling, clear	Gyngle in a whistlyng wynd as cleere,	Jingle along a whistling wind as clear
	And eek as lowde as doth the chapel belle,	And quite as loud, as doth the chapel bell,
where, religious house	Ther as this lord was keper of the selle.	Where this good monk is keeper of the cell.

This jolly monk cared for little else but hunting, though this has never been considered a proper pursuit for the clergy. He was indifferent to what was said of him, and spared no cost to keep the most splendid greyhounds and horses for hard riding and hare-hunting. I saw his sleeves edged with the rare fur *gris* at the wrist, and that the finest in the land; his hood was fastened under his chin with a curious gold pin, which had a love-knot in the largest end. His pate was bald and shiny, his eyes rolled in his head; his favourite roast dish was a fat swan.†

The Friar.

friar	A FRERE ther was, a wantoun and a merye,	A friar there was, so frisky and so merry—
solemn	A lymytour,‡ a ful solempne man.	A limitour, a most important man,
is able to do	In alle the ordres foure § is noon that can	In the four orders there is none that can
dalliance	So moche of daliaunce and fair langage.	Outdo him in sweet talk and playfulness.

. . . .

familiar	Ful wel biloved and famulier was he	He was most intimate and popular
country	With frankeleyns ‖ overal in his cuntre,	With all the franklins dwelling near and far,
also, rich	And eek with worthi wommen of the toun:	And with the wealthy women of the town.

. . . .

* "The custom of hanging small bells on the bridle and harness of horses is still observed on the Continent for the purpose of giving notice to foot-passengers to get out of the way; but it was no doubt often used for ostentation. So Wicliffe inveighs against the clergy in his Triologe for their 'fair hors, and jolly and gay sadels, and bridels ringing by the way.'"

† A bird more commonly eaten in those days than it is now, but expensive even then.

‡ *Lymytour:* a friar licensed to beg within a certain district or limit. This friar, no very pleasing character, is described as making such a good thing out of his begging, that he bribed his fellow friars not to come within his particular haunt, and interfere with his doings: an unprincipled dandy who is another instance of Chaucer's sarcasm against the Church.

§ There were four orders of mendicant friars—Dominicans, Franciscans, Carmelites, and Augustins.

‖ *Frankeleyns:* a franklin was a rich landholder, free of feudal service, holding possessions immediately from the king. See p. 28.

Glossary		
	Ful sweetly herde he confessioun,	So sweetly did he hear confession ay;
	And plesaunt was his absolucioun *	In absolution pleasant was his way.
easy	He was an esy man to yeve penance	In giving penance, very kind was he
when, knew	Ther as he wiste to han a good pitance;	When people made it worth his while to be;
poor	For unto a poure ordre for to geve	For giving largely to some order poor
shriven	Is signe that a man is wel i-schreve.	Shows that a man is free from sin, be sure,
boast	For if he yaf, he dorste make avaunt,	And if a man begrudged him not his dole,
knew	He wiste that a man was repentaunt.	He knew he was repentant in his soul.
heart	For many a man so hard is of his herte,	For many a man so hard of heart we see,
he may smart	He may not wepe though him sore smerte;	He cannot weep, however sad he be;
	Therfore in-stede of wepyng and prayeres,	Therefore, instead of weeping and long prayers,
may	Men moot yive silver to the poure freres.	Men can give money unto the poor friars.

He carried a number of pretty pins and knives about him that he made presents of to people; and he could sing well, and play on the rotta.† He never mingled with poor, ragged, sick people—it is not respectable to have anything to do with such, but only with rich people who could give good dinners.

	Somwhat he lipsede for his wantownesse,	Somewhat he lispéd for his wantonness,
tongue	To make his Englissch swete upon his tunge;	To make his English sweet upon his tongue;

and when he played and sang, his eyes twinkled like the stars on a frosty night.

The Merchant.

beard	A Marchaunt was ther with a forked berd,	A merchant was there with a forkéd beard,
motley, horse	In motteleye, and highe on hors he sat,	In motley dress'd—high on his horse he sat,
Flemish beaver	Uppon his heed a Flaundrisch bevere hat.	And on his head a Flemish beaver hat.

* Confession, absolution, and penance: sacraments in the Roman Catholic Church.

† The rotta was an ancient instrument of the guitar tribe.

The Clerk.

GLOSSARY.

Oxford	A CLERK * ther was of Oxenford also,	A clerk of Oxford was amid the throng,
logic, gone	That unto logik hadde longe ygo.	Who had applied his heart to learning long.
lean, horse	As lene was his hors as is a rake,	His horse, it was as skinny as a rake,
	And he was not right fat, I undertake;	And he was not too fat, I'll undertake!
looked, hollow	But lokede holwe, and therto soburly.	But had a sober, rather hollow look;
uppermost short cloak	Ful thredbare was his overest courtepy.	And very threadbare was his outer cloak.
got	For he hadde geten him yit no benefice,	For he as yet no benefice had got:
	Ne was so worldly for to have office,	Worldly enough for office he was not!
he would	For him was lever have at his beddes heede	For liefer would he have at his bed's head
	Twenty bookes, clothed in blak or reede,	A score of books, all bound in black or red,
	Of Aristotil, and his philosophie,	Of Aristotle, and his philosophy,
robes	Than robus riche, or fithul, or sawtrie.	Than rich attire, fiddle, or psaltery.

Yet although the poor scholar was so wise and diligent, he had hardly any money, but all he could get from his friends he spent on books and on learning; and often he prayed for those who gave him the means to study. He spoke little—never more than he was obliged—but what he did speak was always sensible and wise.

tending to	Sownynge in moral vertu was his speche,	Full of true worth and goodness was his speech,
would, learn	And gladly wolde he lerne, and gladly teche.	And gladly would he learn, and gladly teach.

* *Clerk:* a scholar probably preparing for the priesthood. In many Roman Catholic countries it was the custom till very lately for poor scholars to ask and receive contributions from the people for the expenses of their education. They were often extremely indigent, coming from the labouring classes. The parson, for instance, spoken of later, is said to be brother of the ploughman travelling with him. The poor scholar and the good parson are 'birds of a feather.'

Then there was a

Serjeant-of-Law.

Glossary.		
was not	Nowher so besy a man as he ther nas,	Never has been a busier man than he,
	And yit he seemede besier than he was.	Yet busier than he was, he seemed to be.

. . . .

| mixed fabric } | He roode but hoomly in a medlé coote | He rode but homely-clad, in medley coat, |
| belt | Gird with a seynt of silk, with barres smale. | Girt with a belt of silk, with little bars. |

The Franklin.

The Franklin

Table Dormant

	A Frankelein was in his compainye;	There was a Franklin in his company,
daisy	Whit was his berde, as is the dayesye.	And white his beard was, as the daisies be.
	Of his complexioun he was sangwyn,	With ruddy tints did his complexion shine;
morning	Wel loved he in the morwe a sop of wyn	Well loved he in the morn a sop of wine.

. . . .

baked meats (pies) }	Withoute bake mete was nevere his hous,	Without good meat, well cooked, was ne'er his house,
	Of flessch and fissch, and that so plentevous	Both fish and flesh, and that so plenteous,
snowed	Hit snewed * in his hous of mete and drynke,	It seemed as though it snowed with meat and drink,

* Or, *abounded:* the O. E. *snewe*, like the Prov. Eng. *snee, snie, snive, snew,* signifies *to swarm.*

CHAUCER'S PROLOGUE

GLOSSARY.
could think of — Of alle deyntees that men cowde thynke. — And every dainty that a man could think.
sundry — After the sondry sesouns of the yeer — According to the seasons of the year
supper — So chaungede he his mete and his soper. — He changed his meats and varied his good cheer.

. . . .

His table dormant * in his halle alway — His table-dormant in his hall alway
Stood redy covered al the longe day. — Stood ready furnished forth throughout the day.

He was the most hospitable of men, and very well-to-do. He kept open house, for everybody to come and eat when they liked. He had often been sheriff and knight of the shire; for he was very highly thought of.

all — An anlas and gipser al of silk — A dagger and a hawking-pouch of silk
Heng at his gerdul, whit as morne mylk. — Hung at his girdle, white as morning milk.

A Haberdasher, a Carpenter, a Webber (weaver), a Dyer, and a Tapiser (tapestry-maker) came next,

The Doctor of Physic

The Wife of Bath

with the Cook they brought with them, a Shipman, a Doctor of Physic, and a 'worthy † woman,' called the Wife of Bath, because she lived near that city.

𝕿𝖍𝖊 𝕻𝖗𝖎𝖔𝖗𝖊𝖘𝖘.

She was so expert in weaving cloth, that there was no one who could come up to her; and she thought so much of herself, that if another woman even went up to the church altar before her, she considered it a slight upon her. The Wife of Bath was middle-aged, and somewhat deaf: she had had five husbands, but they had all died—she was such a shrew: and she had taken pilgrimages to Cologne and Rome, and many other places; for she had plenty of money, as one might see by her showy dress.

---

* The table dormant was a permanent table, not a board on trestles such as the ordinary one, mentioned on p. 2. It was only used by very rich people, for it was a new fashion, and expensive. See drawing of table dormant in 14th century, on page 28.

† Well-to-do.

hose	Hire hosen weren of fyn scarlet reed,	Her stockings were of finest scarlet red,
	Ful streyte yteyd, and schoos ful moyst and newe.	All straitly tied, and shoes all moist and new.
	Bold was hire face, and fair and rede of hew.	Bold was her face, and fair and red of hue.

She was well wimpled with fine kerchiefs, and her hat was as broad as a buckler or a target.

The Parson.

Then came the poor Parson—poor in condition, but 'rich in holy thought and work'—who was so good, and staunch, and true, so tender to sinners and severe to sin, regarding no ranks or state, but always at his post, an example to men.

wide	Wyd was his parisch, and houses fer asondur,	Wide was his parish, the houses far asunder,
ceased	But he ne lafte not for reyne ne thondur,	But never did he fail, for rain or thunder,
	In siknesse nor in meschief to visite	In sickness and in woe to visit all
furthest	The ferrest in his parissche, moche and lite,	Who needed—far or near, and great and small—
	Uppon his feet, and in his hond a staf.	On foot, and having in his hand a staff.
	. . . .	. . . .
	But Cristes lore and his apostles twelve	Christ's and the twelve apostles' law he taught,
followed	He taught, and ferst he folwed it himselve. *	But first himself obey'd it, as he ought.

The Ploughman.

Then the parson's brother, who was only a Ploughman, and worked hard in the fields, kind to his neighbours, ever honest, loving God above all things. He wore a tabard, and rode on a mare. †

---

* Chaucer speaks, you see, in very different terms of the poor and conscientious parish priest (who was supported only by his benefice and tithes of the people—a small income) from what he does of the monastic orders, corrupted by the wealth they had accumulated. Bell says—"It was quite natural that Chaucer, the friend of John of Gaunt, should praise the parochial clergy, who were poor, and therefore not formidable, at the expense of the rich monastic orders who formed the only barriers which then existed against the despotic power of the aristocracy." But, however that may be, there is no doubt that these parish parsons actually were a much better and more honest class of men than the monks, and the begging friars, and all the rest, were at this time. They were drawn, like the Roman Catholic secular clergy of the present day, from the labouring classes.

† No one of good position rode on a mare in the middle ages.

The Ploughman   The Summoner   The Pardoner

𝕿𝖍𝖊 𝕾𝖚𝖒𝖒𝖔𝖓𝖊𝖗.

The Summoner * was a terrible-looking person, and rode with the Pardoner, who was his friend: the Pardoner singing a lively song, and the Summoner growling out a bass to it, with a loud, harsh voice. As for his looks, he had

GLOSSARY.

                  A fyr-reed cherubynes face, †   A 'fiery-cherubin' red face,

pimply   For sawceflem he was with eyghen narwe.   For pimply he was, with narrow eyes.

Children were sore afraid of him when they saw him, he was so repulsive, and so cruel in extorting his gains. He was a very bad man: for though it was his duty to call up before the Archdeacon's court anybody whom he found doing wrong, yet he would let the wickedest people off, if they bribed him with money; and many poor people who did nothing wrong he forced to give him their hard earnings, threatening else to report them falsely to the Archdeacon. He carried a large cake with him for a buckler, and wore a garland big enough for the sign-post of an inn. ‡

𝕿𝖍𝖊 𝕻𝖆𝖗𝖉𝖔𝖓𝖊𝖗.

The Pardoner § was a great cheat too, and so the friends were well matched; he had long thin hair, as yellow as wax, that hung in shreds on his shoulders. He wore no hood, but kept it in his wallet: he thought himself quite in the tip-top of fashion.

* *Summoner:* an officer employed by the ecclesiastical courts to summon any persons who broke the law to appear before the archdeacon, who imposed what penalty he thought fit. The Summoners found it to their interest to accept bribes not to report offences: therefore bad people who could afford to pay got off, whilst those who could not afford to pay were punished with rigour. Many Summoners extorted bribes by threatening to say people had transgressed the law who had *not;* and so they got to be detested by the masses, and Chaucer's hideous picture gives the popular notion of a Summoner.

† A face as red as the fiery cherubin: a rather profane simile! In many ancient pictures we find the cherubin painted wholly scarlet; and the term had become a proverb. 'Sawceflem' is from *salsum flegma,* a disease of the skin.

‡ See note, p. 92, note * .

§ *Pardoner:* Seller of the Pope's indulgences.

Glossary		
except	Dischevele, sauf his cappe, he rood al bare.	Dishevell'd, save his cap, he rode barehead:
such, eyes	Suche glaryng eyghen hadde he, as an hare.	Such glaring eyes, like to a hare, he had!
	A vernicle * hadde he sowed on his cappe;	A vernicle was sewed upon his cap;
before	His walet lay byforn him in his lappe.	His wallet lay before him, in his lap.

. . . .

truly	But trewely to tellen atte laste,	But honestly to tell the truth at last,
	He was in churche a noble ecclesiaste.	He was in church a noble ecclesiast.
	Wel cowde he rede a lessoun or a storye,†	Well could he read a lesson or a story,
best of all	But altherbest he sang an offertorie:	But ever best he sang the offertory:
knew, when	For wel he wyste, whan that song was songe	For well he knew that after he had sung,
preach, whet	He moste preche, and wel affyle his tonge,	For preaching he must polish up his tongue,
win	To wynne silver, as he right wel cowde:	And thus make money, as he right well could:
	Therfore he sang ful meriely and lowde.	Therefore he sang full merrily and loud.

Now I have told you as much as I can what people came into the Tabard Inn that night, and why they were all travelling together, and where they were going.

Mine Host

Our host made us very welcome, and gave us a capital supper. He was a thoroughly good fellow, our host—a large, stout man, with bright, prominent eyes, sensible and well behaved, and very merry.

After supper, he made us all laugh a good deal with his witty jests; and when we had all paid our reckonings, he addressed us all:—

truly	And sayde thus: Lo, lordynges, trewely	And said to us: "My masters, certainly
	Ye ben to me right welcome hertily:	Ye be to me right welcome, heartily:
shall, lie	For by my trouthe, if that I schal not lye,	For by my truth, and flattering none, say I,
saw	I ne saugh this yeer so mery a companye	I have not seen so large a company
inn (auberge)	At oones in this herbergh, as is now.	At once inside my inn this year, as now!
	Fayn wolde I do yow merthe, wiste I how.	I'd gladly make you mirth if I knew how.

* A vernicle—diminutive of *Veronike*—was a small copy of the face of Christ, worn as a token that he had just returned from a pilgrimage to Rome.

† The Pardoner's eloquence and musical gifts account, perhaps, for the exquisite story he afterwards tells.

Glossary.		
	And of a merthe I am right now bythought,	And of a pleasant game I'm just bethought
do, ease	To doon you eese, and it schal coste nought.	To cheer the journey—it shall cost you nought!

"Whoever wants to know how, hold up your hands." We all held up our hands, and begged him to say on.

"Well, my masters," said he, "I say that each of you shall tell the rest four stories—two on the way to Canterbury, and two on the way home. For you know it is small fun riding along as dumb as a stone. And whichever in the party tells the best story, shall have a supper at this inn at the cost of the rest when you come back. To amuse you better, I will myself gladly join your party, and ride to Canterbury at my own expense, and be at once guide and judge; and whoever gainsays my judgment shall pay for all we spend by the way. Now, tell me if you all agree, and I will get me ready in time to start."

We were all well pleased; and the next morning, at daybreak, our clever host called us all together, and we rode off to a place called the Watering of St. Thomas. * There we halted, and drew lots who should tell the story first, knight, clerk, lady prioress, and everybody.

The lot fell to the knight, which every one was glad of; and as soon as we set forward, he began at once.

Notes by the Way.

ONE of the things most deserving of notice in reading Chaucer is his singularly strong grasp of character. In the 'Canterbury Tales' this is self-evident, and the succinct catalogue of the thirty-one pilgrims, which in feebler hands would have been dry enough, is a masterpiece of good-humoured satire, moral teaching, and, above all, photographic portraits from life. You will notice that Chaucer meant to make his 'Canterbury Tales' much longer than he lived to do. His innkeeper proposes that each of the pilgrims shall tell four stories. Only twenty-four of these exist.

You will never find any character drawn by Chaucer acting, speaking, or looking inconsistently. He has always well hold of his man, and he turns him inside out relentlessly. He very seldom analyzes thought or motives, but he shows you what *is* so clearly, that you know what *must* be without his telling you.

The good-humoured *naïveté* of mine host, like all his class, never forgetful of business in the midst of play, is wonderfully well hit off; for the innkeeper clearly would be the gainer by this pleasant stratagem: and he prevents any one's giving him the slip by going with them to Canterbury and back. The guests are glad enough of his company, for he could be especially useful to them on the way.

The stories, also, will be found perfectly characteristic of the tellers—there is no story given to a narrator whose rank, education, or disposition make it inconsistent. Each tells a tale whose incidents savour of his natural occupation and sympathies, and the view each takes of right or wrong modes of conduct is well seen in the manner as well as the matter.

Chaucer's personal distrust of and contempt for the contemporary Church and its creatures was the natural and healthy aversion of a pure mind and a sincerely religious heart to a form of godliness denying the power thereof—a Church which had become really corrupt. It is significant of his perfect artistic thoroughness that, with this aversion, he never puts an immoral or unfitting tale into the mouth of nun or friar; for it would be most unlikely that these persons, whatever their private character might be, would criminate themselves in public.

* Mr. Wright says this place was situated at the second milestone on the old Canterbury road.

The Knight's Tale.

ONCE upon a time, as old stories tell us, there was a duke named Theseus, lord and governor of Athens, in Greece, and in his time such a conqueror that there was none greater under the sun. Full many a rich country owned his sway.

GLOSSARY.

	That with his wisdam and his chivalrie,	What with his wisdom and his chivalry
kingdom, Amazons	He conquered al the regne of Femynye,	The kingdom of the Amazons won he,
once, called	That whilom was i-cleped Cithea;	That was of old time naméd Scythia,
fresh	And wedded the fresshe quene Ipolita,	And wedded the fresh Queen Ipolita,
country	And brought her hoom with him to his contre,	And brought her to his own land sumptuously,
much, solemnity	With mochel glorie and gret solempnite;	With pomp and glory, and great festivity;
also, sister	And eek hire yonge suster Emelye.	And also her young sister Emelye.
music	And thus with victorie and with melodye	And thus with victory and with melodie
duke	Lete I this noble duk to Athenes ryde,	Let I this noble duke to Athens ride,
arms	And al his ost, in armes him biside.	And all his glittering hosts on either side.

And, certainly, if it were not too long to listen to, I would have told you fully how the kingdom of the Amazons was won by Theseus and his host. And of the great battle there was for the time between Athens and the Amazons; and how Ipolita—the fair, hardy queen of Scythia—was besieged; and about the feast that was held at the wedding of Theseus and Ipolita, and about the tempest at their home-coming. But all this I must cut short.

plough	I have, God wot, a large feeld to ere;	I have, God knows, a full wide field to sow,
weak	And wayke ben the oxen in my plough.	And feeble be the oxen in my plough.

I will not hinder anybody in the company. Let every one tell his story in turn, and let us see now who shall win the supper!

I will describe to you what happened as Theseus was bringing home his bride to Athens.

✱ Tyrwhitt. Hyppolita, Smith's Dic.

THE KNIGHT'S TALE

Glossary.		
	This duk, of whom I make mencioun,	This duke aforesaid, of deserved renown,
come	Whan he was comen almost unto the toun,	When he had almost come into the town
prosperity	In al his wele and in his moste pryde,	In all his splendour and in all his pride,
aware	He was war, as he cast his eyghe aside,	Perceivéd, as he cast his eyes aside,
kneeled	Wher that ther knelede in the hye weye	A company of ladies, in a row,
two	A compagnye of ladies, tweye and tweye,	Were kneeling in the highway—two by two,
each, black	Ech after other, clad in clothes blake;	Each behind each, clad all in black array;
woe	But such a cry and such a woo they make,	But such an outcry of lament made they,
	That in this world nys creature lyvynge,	That in this world there is no living thing
	That herde such another weymentynge,	That e'er heard such another outcrying;
cease	And of that cry ne wolde they never stenten,	Nor would they cease to wail and to complain
caught	Til they the reynes of his bridel henten.	Till they had caught him by his bridle-rein.
	What folk be ye that at myn hom comynge	"What folk are ye who at my home-coming
perturb	Pertourben so my feste * with crynge?	Perturb my festival with murmuring,"
	Quod Theseus; Have ye so gret envye	Quoth Theseus. "Or do you envy me
	Of myn honour, that thus compleyne and crie?	Mine honour that ye wail so woefully?
injured	Or who hath yow misboden or offendid?	Or who hath injured you, or who offended?
	And telleth me, if it may ben amendid;	Tell me, if haply it may be amended,
black	And why that ye ben clad thus al in blak?	And why are all of you in black arrayed?"
them	The oldest lady of hem alle spak....	The oldest lady of them all then said—

"Lord, to whom fortune has given victory, and to live ever as a conqueror, we do not grudge your glory † and honour, but we have come to implore your pity and help. Have mercy on us in our grief. There is not one of us that has not been a queen or duchess; now we are beggars, and you can help us if you will.

"I was wife to King Capaneus, who died at Thebes ‡ : and all of us who kneel and weep have lost our husbands there during a siege; and now Creon, who is king of Thebes, has piled together these dead bodies, and will not suffer them to be either burned or buried."

And with these words all the ladies wept more piteously than ever, and prayed Theseus to have compassion on their great sorrow.

The kind duke descended from his horse, full of commiseration for the poor ladies. He thought his heart would break with pity when he saw them so sorrowful and dejected, who had been lately of so noble a rank.

He raised them all, and comforted them, and swore an oath that as he was a true knight, he would avenge them on the tyrant king of Thebes in such a fashion that all the people of Greece should be able to tell how Theseus served Creon!

The duke sent his royal bride and her young sister Emelye on to the town of Athens, whilst he

---

* Feste in this place means rather festival than feast, as Theseus was only on his way to the city.

† At this period, the personal pronoun *you* was used only in the plural sense, or in formal address, as on the Continent now; whilst *thou* implied familiarity. The Deity, or any superior, was therefore addressed as *you*: intimates and inferiors as *thou*. Throughout Chaucer the distinction is noticeable: but as the present mode reverses the order, I have in my lines adhered to no strict principle, but have used the singular or plural personal pronoun according as it seemed most forcible.

‡ Thebes, in Greece.

displayed his banner, marshalled his men, and rode forth towards Thebes. For himself, till he had accomplished this duty, he would not enter Athens, nor take his ease for one half-day therein.

The duke's white banner bore the red statue of Mars upon it; and by his banner waved his pennon, which had the monster Minotaur (slain by Theseus in Greece) beaten into it in gold. Thus rode this duke—thus rode this conqueror and all his host—the flower of chivalry—till he came to Thebes.

To make matters short, Theseus fought with the King of Thebes, and slew him manly as a knight in fair battle, and routed his whole army. Then he destroyed the city, and gave up to the sorrowful ladies the bones of their husbands, to burn honourably after their fashion.

When the worthy duke had slain Creon and taken the city, he remained all night in the field. During the pillage which followed, it happened that two young knights were found still alive, lying in their rich armour, though grievously wounded. By their coat-armour* the heralds knew they were of the blood-royal of Thebes; two cousins, the sons of two sisters. Their names were Palamon and Arcite.

These two knights were carried as captives to Theseus' tent, and he sent them off to Athens, where they were to be imprisoned for life; no ransom would he take.

Then the duke went back to Athens crowned with laurel, where he lived in joy and in honour all his days, while Palamon and Arcite were shut up in a strong tower full of anguish and misery, beyond all reach of help.

Thus several years passed.

Glossary.		
	This passeth yeer by yeer, and day by day,	Thus passeth year by year, and day by day,
morning	Till it fel oones in a morwe of May	Till it fell once upon a morn of May
see	That Emelye, that fairer was to seene	That Emelye—more beauteous to be seen
	Than is the lilie on hire stalkes grene,	Than is the lily on his stalk of green,
flowers	And fresscher than the May with floures newe—	And fresher than the May with flowers new
strove, hue	For with the rose colour strof hire hewe,	(For with the rose's colour strove her hue
	I n'ot which was the fayrere of hem two—	I know not which was fairer of the two)
	Er it were day as sche was wont to do,	Early she rose as she was wont to do,
dressed	Sche was arisen, and al redy dight;	All ready robed before the day was bright;
sloth	For May wole han no sloggardye a nyght.	For May time will not suffer sloth at night;
	The sesoun priketh every gentil herte,	The season pricketh every gentle heart,
	And maketh him out of his sleepe sterte,	And maketh him out of his sleep to start,
arise, thine	And seith, Arys, and do thin observaunce.†	And saith, Rise up, salute the birth of spring!

* A garment worn over the armour, on which the armorial bearings were usually embroidered, for the purpose of recognition. See *tabard*, p. 48.

† The rites and ceremonies, observed on the approach of spring, from the earliest times in many countries, but which have now died out in England, are among the most natural and beautiful of all popular fêtes. I have already in the preface alluded to the custom of riding out into the fields at daybreak to do honour to May, the month which was held to be the symbol of spring-time. Rich and poor, the court and the commoners, all rode out with one impulse. Boughs of hawthorn and laburnum were brought home to decorate all the streets, and dancing round the maypole, and feasting, and holiday-making, were observed almost like religious rites. It was a great privilege to be elected queen of May, and one which every young maiden coveted. At a later time we read of Henry VIII. and Queen Catherine of Aragon formally meeting the heads of the corporation of London, on Shooter's Hill, to 'go a maying.'

But one thing should be remembered when we see how many pleasures were referred to May, and how much more people seemed to count on the weather of a month nowadays proverbially disappointing. The seasons were not the same then as they are now. Not because the climate of the land has altered so much, though that may be fairly surmised; but because the seasons were actually arranged otherwise. In Chaucer's time, May began twelve days later than our May, and ended in the midst of June, and therefore there was a much better chance of settled weather than we have. This fact also accounts for the proverbial connection of Christmas and hard weather, snow, and ice, which *we* get as a rule in January, while December is foggy and wet. Twelfth Day was the old Christmas Day. (See page 4.)

FAIR EMELYE GATHERING FLOWERS

'The fairnesse of the lady that I see
Yonde in the gardyn romynge to and fro.'

Glossary.		
	This maked Emelye han remembraunce	And therefore Emelye, remembering
do	To don honour to May, and for to ryse.	To pay respect to May, rose speedily:
clothed	I-clothed was sche fressh for to devyse. *	Attired she was all fresh and carefully,
yellow	Hire yolwe heer was browdid in a tresse,	Her yellow hair was braided in a tress
	Byhynde hire bak, a yerde long I gesse.	Behind her back, a full yard long, I guess,
	And in the gardyn at the sonne upriste	And in the garden as the sun uprose
pleased	Sche walketh up and doun wher as hire liste.	She wandered up and down where as she chose.
	Sche gadereth floures, party whyte and reede,	She gathereth flowers, partly white and red,
	To make a sotil gerland † for hire heede,	To make a cunning garland for her head,
	And as an aungel hevenly sche song.	And as an angel heavenly she sang.

The great tower, so thick and strong, in which these two knights were imprisoned, was close-joined to the wall of the garden.

Bright was the sun, and clear, that morning, as Palamon, by leave of his jailor, had risen, and was roaming about in an upper chamber, from which he could see the whole noble city of Athens, and also the garden, full of green boughs, just where fresh Emelye was walking.

This sorrowful prisoner, this Palamon, kept pacing to and fro in this chamber, wishing he had never been born; and it happened by chance that through the window, square and barred with iron, he cast his eyes on Emelye.

He started and cried out aloud, "Ah!" as though he were stricken to the heart.

And with that cry Arcite sprang up, saying, "Dear cousin, what ails you? You are quite pale and deathly. Why did you cry out? For God's love be patient with this prison life since it cannot be altered. What is Heaven's will we must endure."

Palamon answered, "Cousin, it is not that—not this dungeon made me cry out—but I was smitten right now through the eye into my heart. The fairness of a lady that I see yonder in the garden, roaming to and fro, made me cry out. I know not whether she be woman or goddess: but I think it is Venus herself!"

And he fell down on his knees and cried, "Venus, if it be thy will thus to transfigure thyself in the garden, help us to escape out of the tower."

Then Arcite looked forth and saw this lady roaming to and fro, and her beauty touched him so deeply that he said, sighing, "The fresh beauty of her will slay me. And if I cannot gain her mercy, I am but dead, and there is an end."

But Palamon turned furiously on him, and said, "Do you say that in earnest or in play?"

"Nay," cried Arcite, "in earnest by my faith—God help me, I am in no mood for play."

"It were no great honour to thee," cried Palamon, "to be false and a traitor to me, who am thy cousin and thy brother, sworn as we are both, to help and not hinder one another, in all things till death part us. And now you would falsely try to take my lady from me, whom I love and serve, and ever shall till my heart break. Now, certainly, false Arcite, you shall not do it. I loved her first, and told thee, and thou art bound as a knight to help me, or thou art false!"

But Arcite answered proudly, "Thou shalt be rather false than I—and thou *art* false, I tell thee,

---

* At point devise—with exactness.

† The love of the Anglo-Saxons and the early English for flowers is very remarkable. The wearing of garlands of fresh flowers was a common practice with both sexes: a beautiful custom, followed by the Romans, and previously by the Greeks.

utterly! For I loved her with real love before you did. You did not know whether she were woman or goddess. Yours is a religious feeling, and mine is love as to a mortal; which I told you as my cousin, and my sworn brother. And even if you *had* loved her first, what matters it? A man loves because he can't help it, not because he wishes. Besides, you will never gain her grace more than I, for both of us are life-long captives. It is like the dogs who fought all day over a bone; and while they were fighting over it, a kite came and carried it off."

Long the two knights quarrelled and disputed about the lady who was out of their reach. But you shall see what came to pass.

There was a duke called Perithous, who had been fellow and brother in arms * of Duke Theseus since both were children, and he came to Athens to visit Theseus. These two dukes were very great friends: so much so that they loved no one so much as each other.

Now, Duke Perithous had known Arcite at Thebes, years before, and liked him, and he begged Theseus to let Arcite out of prison.

Theseus consented, but only on the condition that Arcite should quit Athens; and that he should lose his head, were he ever found there again.

So Arcite became a free man, but he was banished the kingdom.

How unhappy then Arcite was! He felt that he was worse off than ever. "Oh, how I wish I had never known Perithous!" cried he. "Far rather would I be back in Theseus' prison, for *then* I could see the beautiful lady I love."

GLOSSARY.

thine, chance
may'st
thou
endure

thee

O dere cosyn Palamon, quod he,	"O my dear cousin, Palamon," cried he,
Thyn is the victorie of this aventure,	"In this ill hap the gain is on thy side.
Ful blisfully in prisoun maistow dure;	Thou blissful in thy prison may'st abide!
In prisoun? certes nay, but in paradys!	In prison? truly nay—but in paradise!
Wel hath fortune y-torned the the dys.	Kindly toward thee hath fortune turn'd the dice."

So Arcite mourned ever, because he was far away from Athens where the beautiful lady dwelt, and was always thinking that perhaps Palamon would get pardoned, and marry the lady, while he would never see her any more.

But Palamon, on the other hand, was so unhappy when his companion was taken away, that he wept till the great tower resounded, and his very fetters were wet with his tears.

"Alas, my dear cousin," he sighed, "the fruit of all our strife is thine!—You walk free in Thebes, and think little enough of my woe, I daresay. You will perhaps gather a great army and make war on this country, and get the beautiful lady to wife whom I love so much! while I die by inches in my cage."

And with that his jealousy started up like a fire within him, so that he was nigh mad, and pale as ashes. "O cruel gods!" he cried, "that govern the world with your eternal laws, how is man better than a sheep lying in the fold? For, like any other beast, man dies, or lives in prison, or is sick, or unfortunate, and often is quite guiltless all the while. And when a beast is dead, it has no pain further; but man may suffer after death, as well as in this world."

Now I will leave Palamon, and tell you more of Arcite.

---

* Formal compacts for the purpose of mutual counsel and assistance were common to the heroic and chivalrous ages.—B.

Arcite, in Thebes, fell into such excessive sorrow for the loss of the beautiful lady that there never was a creature so sad before or since. He ceased to eat and drink, and sleep, and grew as thin and dry as an arrow. His eyes were hollow and dreadful to behold, and he lived always alone, mourning and lamenting night and day. He was so changed that no one could recognize his voice nor his look. Altogether he was the saddest picture of a man that ever was seen—except Palamon.

One night he had a dream. He dreamed that the winged god Mercury stood before him, bidding him be merry; and commanded him to go to Athens, where all his misery should end.

Arcite sprang up, and said, "I will go straight to Athens. Nor will I spare to see my lady through fear of death—in her presence I am ready even to die!"

He caught up a looking-glass, and saw how altered his face was, so that no one would know him. And he suddenly bethought him that now he was so disfigured with his grief, he might go and dwell in Athens without being recognized, and see his lady nearly every day.

He dressed himself as a poor labourer, and accompanied only by a humble squire, who knew all he had suffered, he hastened to Athens.

He went to the court of Theseus, and offered his services at the gate to drudge and draw, or do any menial work that could be given him. Well could he hew wood and carry water, for he was young and very strong. Now, it happened that the chamberlain of fair Emelye's house took Arcite into his service.

Thus Arcite became page of the chamber of Emelye the bright, and he called himself Philostrate.

Never was man so well thought of!—he was so gentle of condition that he became known throughout the court. People said it would be but right if Theseus promoted this Philostrate, and placed him in a rank which would better display his talents and virtues.

At last Theseus raised him to be squire of his chamber, and gave him plenty of gold to keep up his degree. Moreover, his own private rent was secretly brought to him from Thebes year by year. But he spent it so cunningly that no one suspected him. In this crafty way Arcite lived a long time very happily, and bore himself so nobly both in peace and war that there was no man in the land dearer to Theseus.

Now we will go back to Palamon.

Poor Palamon had been for seven years in his terrible prison, and was quite wasted away with misery. There was not the slightest chance of getting out; and his great love made him frantic. At last, however, one May night some pitying friend helped him to give his jailor a drink which sent him into a deep sleep: so that Palamon made his escape from the tower. He fled from the city as fast as ever he could go, and hid himself in a grove; meaning afterwards to go by night secretly to Thebes, and beg all his friends to aid him to make war on Theseus. And then he would soon either die or get Emelye to wife.

GLOSSARY.

turn	Now wol I torn unto Arcite agayn,	Now will I tell you of Arcite again,
knew, near	That litel wiste how nyh that was his care,	Who little guess'd how nigh him was his care
	Til that fortune hadde brought him in the snare.	Until his fortune brought him in the snare.
	The busy larke, messager of day,	The busy lark, the messenger of day,
saluteth	Salueth in hire song the morwe gray;	Saluteth in her song the morning grey;
	And fyry Phebus ryseth up so brighte,	And fiery Phœbus riseth up so bright,
	That al the orient laugheth of the lighte,	That all the orient laugheth for the light;

GOLDEN KEY TO CHAUCER

GLOSSARY.

rays, groves	And with his stremes dryeth in the greves	And in the woods he drieth with his rays
leaves	The silver dropes, hongyng on the leeves.	The silvery drops that hang along the sprays.
royal*	And Arcite, that is in the court ryal	Arcite—unknown, yet ever waxing higher
squire	With Theseus, his squyer principal,	In Theseus' royal court, now chiefest squire—
	Is risen, and loketh on the merye day.	Is risen, and looketh on the merry day:
do, ceremony	And for to doon his observaunce to May,	And, fain to offer homage unto May,
	Remembryng on the poynt of his desir,	He, mindful of the point of his desire,
starting, fire	He on his courser, stertyng as the fir,	Upon his courser leapeth, swift as fire,
fields, play	Is riden into the feeldes him to pleye	And rideth to keep joyous holiday
	Out of the court, were it a myle or tweye.	Out in the fields, a mile or two away.
you	And to the grove of which that I yow tolde,	And, as it chanced, he made towards the grove,
chance, began	By aventure his wey he gan to holde,	All thick with leaves, whereof I spake above,
make	To maken him a garland of the greves,	Eager to weave a garland with a spray
leaves	Were it of woodebynde or hawethorn leves,	Of woodbine, or the blossoms of the may.
sang, against	And lowde he song ayens the sonne scheene:	And loud against the sunshine sweet he sings,
	O May,† with al thy floures and thy grene,	"O May, with all thy flowers and thy green things,
	Welcome be thou, wel faire freissche May!	Right welcome be thou, fairest, freshest May!
some, may get	I hope that I som grene gete may.	Yield me of all thy tender green to-day!"
heart	And fro his courser, with a lusty herte,	Then from his courser merrily he sprang,
started	Into the grove ful hastily he sterte,	And plunged into the thicket as he sang;
roamed	And in a pathe he romed up and doun,	Till in a path he chanced to make his way
where, chance	Ther as by aventure this Palamoun	Nigh to where Palamon in secret lay.
	Was in a busche, that no man might him see,	Sore frighted for his life was Palamon:
afraid, death	For sore afered of his deth was he.	But Arcite pass'd, unknowing and unknown;
	Nothing ne knew he that it was Arcite:	And neither guess'd his brother was hard by;
knows, guessed, little	God wot he wolde han trowed it ful lite.	But Arcite knew not any man was nigh.
truly, gone, since	For soth is seyd, goon sithen many yeres,	So was it said of old, how faithfully,
eyes, ears	That feld hath eyen, and the woode hath eeres.	'The woods have ears, the empty field can see.'

A man should be prudent, even when he fancies himself safest: for oftentimes come unlooked-for meetings. And little enough thought Arcite that his sworn brother from the tower was at hand, sitting as still as a mouse while he sang.

Whan that Arcite hadde romed al his fill,	Now when Arcite long time had roam'd his fill,
And songen al the roundel lustily,	And sung all through the rondel lustily,

* The words *court* and *royal*, now applied only to the sovereign of the land, were applicable then to the domains of the great nobles, who were to all intents and purposes kings. Their pride, and wealth, and immense power, made them very formidable to the sovereign, as we constantly find in following the history of England or any other country. They often mustered as big an army as the king, because they could afford to pay the knights (see note, p. 19), and were invincible in their strongholds, surrounded by their serfs dependent on them.

† Tyrwhitt.

THE KNIGHT'S TALE

Glossary		
reverie	Into a studie he fel sodeynly,	He fell into dejection suddenly,
curious fashions	As don thes loveres in here queynte geeres,	As lovers in their strange way often do,
briars	Now in the croppe,* now doun in the breres,	Now in the clouds and now in abject wo,
	Now up, now doun, as boket in a welle.	Now up, now down, as bucket in a well.

He sat down and began to make a kind of song of lamentation. "Alas," he cried, "the day that I was born! How long, O Juno, wilt thou oppress Thebes? All her royal blood is brought to confusion. I myself am of royal lineage, and yet now I am so wretched and brought so low, that I have become slave and squire to my mortal foe. Even my own proud name of Arcite I dare not bear, but pass by the worthless one of Philostrate! Ah, Mars and Juno, save me, and wretched Palamon, martyred by Theseus in prison! For all my pains are for my love's sake, and Emelye, whom I will serve all my days."

	Ye slen me with youre eyen, Emelye;	"You slay me with your eyes, O Emelye!
be	Ye ben the cause wherfore that I dye:	You are the cause wherefore I daily die.
remnant	Of al the remenant of myn other care	For, ah, the worth of all my other woes
amount	Ne sette I nought the mountaunce of a tare,	Is not as e'en the poorest weed that grows,
were able to	So that I couthe don aught to youre pleasaunce!	So that I might do aught to pleasure you!"

Palamon, hearing this, felt as though a cold sword glided through his heart. He was so angry that he flung himself forth like a madman upon Arcite:—

	And seyde: False† Arcyte—false traitour wikke,	Crying, "False, wicked traitor! false Arcite!
wicked		
	Now art thou hent, that lovest my lady so,	Now art thou caught, that lov'st my lady so,
	For whom that I have al this peyne and wo,	For whom I suffer all this pain and wo!
counsel	And art my blood, and to my counseil sworn,	Yet art my blood—bound to me by thy vow,
before now	As I ful ofte have told the heere byforn,	As I have told thee oftentimes ere now—
tricked	And hast byjaped here duke Theseus,	And hast so long befool'd Duke Theseus
	And falsly chaunged hast thy name thus;	And falsely hid thy name and nurture thus!
dead, else	I wol be deed, or elles thou schalt dye.	For all this falseness thou or I must die.
	Thou schalt not love my lady Emelye,	Thou shalt not love my lady Emelye—
more	But I wil love hire oonly and no mo;	But I will love her and no man but I,
foe	For I am Palamon, thy mortal fo.	For I am Palamon, thine enemy!
weapon	And though that I no wepne have in this place,	And tho' I am unarmed, being but now
escaped	But out of prisoun am astert by grace,	Escap'd from out my dungeon, care not thou,
fear	I drede not, that outher thou schalt dye,	For nought I dread—for either thou shalt die
	Or thou ne schalt not loven Emelye.	Now—or thou shalt not love my Emelye.
escape	Ches which thou wilt, for thou schalt not sterte.	Choose as thou wilt—thou shalt not else depart."
there	This Arcite, with ful dispitous herte,	But Arcite, with all fury in his heart,

---

* *Crop*, the top of the wood; *briars*, the thorny brushwood and weeds growing on the ground. This pretty metaphor well expresses the fluctuating moods of an overwrought state of feeling. † Tyrwhitt.

Glossary		
	Whan he him knew, and hadde his tale herde,	Now that he knew him and his story heard,
fierce	As fers as a lyoun, pulleth out a swerde,	Fierce as a lion, snatch'd he forth his sword,
	And seide thus: By God that sitteth above,	Saying these words: "By Him who rules above,
were it not	Nere it that thou art sike and wood for love,	Were't not that thou art sick and mad for love,
also	And eek that thou no wepne hast in this place,	And hast no weapon—never should'st thou move,
step	Thou schuldest nevere out of this grove pace,	Living or like to live, from out this grove,
die	That thou ne schuldest deyen of myn hond.	But thou shouldest perish by my hand! on oath
defy	For I defye the seurté and the bond	I cast thee back the bond and surety, both,
sayest	Which that thou seyst that I have maad to the;	Which thou pretendest I have made to thee.
	What, verray fool, thenk wel that love is fre!	What? very fool! remember love is free,
In spite of	And I wol love hire mawgré al thy might.	And I will love her maugré all thy might!
because	But, for thou art a gentil perfight knight,	But since thou art a worthy, noble knight,
art willing	And wilnest to dereyne hire by batayle,	And willing to contest her in fair fight,
pledge	Have heere my trouthe, to morwe I nyl not fayle,	Have here my troth, to-morrow, at daylight,
without knowledge	Withouten wityng of eny other wight,	Unknown to all, I will not fail nor fear
will, found	That heer I wol be founden as a knight,	To meet thee as a knight in combat here,
	And bryngen harneys * right inough for the;	And I will bring full arms for me and thee;
	And ches the best, and lef the worst for me.	And choose the best, and leave the worst for me!
	And mete and drynke this night wil I brynge	And I will bring thee meat and drink to-night,
	Inough for the, and clothes for thy beddynge.	Enough for thee, and bedding as is right:
win	And if so be that thou my lady wynne,	And if the victory fall unto thine hand,
wood	And sle me in this wode, ther I am inne,	To slay me in this forest where I stand,
	Thou maist wel have thy lady as for me.	Thou may'st attain thy lady-love, for me!"
	This Palamon answerde, I graunt it the.	Then Palamon replied—"I grant it thee."

Then these, who had once been friends, parted till the morrow.

all	O Cupide, out of alle charite!	O god of love, that hast no charity!
kingdom	O regne that wolt no felaw have with the!	O realm, that wilt not bear a rival nigh!
truly, nor	Ful soth is seyd, that love ne lordschipe	Truly 'tis said, that love and lordship ne'er
willingly, fellowship	Wol not, his thonkes, have no felaschipe.	Will be contented only with a share.
find	Wel fynden that Arcite and Palamoun.	Arcite and Palamon have found it so.
	Arcite is riden anon unto the toun	Arcite is ridden soon the town unto:
before	And on the morwe, or it were dayes light,	And, on the morrow, ere the sun was high,
prepared	Ful prively two harneys hath he dight,	Two harness hath he brought forth privily,
sufficient	Bothe suffisaunt and mete to darreyne	Meet and sufficing for the lonely fight
field, them, two	The batayl in the feeld betwix hem tweyne.	Out in the battle-field mid daisies white.
carried	And on his hors alone as he was born,	And riding onward solitarily

* Harness was a technical term for the complete armour or equipment, as opposed to portions, which were equally *armour*.

Glossary		
before	He caryed al this harneys him byforn;	All this good armour on his horse bore he:
	And in the grove, at tyme and place i-sette,	And at the time and place which they had set
be	This Arcite and this Palamon ben mette.	Ere long Arcite and Palamon are met.
then, their	Tho chaungen gan here colour in here face,	To change began the colour of each face—
kingdom	Right as the honter in the regne of Trace	Ev'n as the hunter's, in the land of Thrace,
	That stondeth in the gappe with a spere,	When at a gap he standeth with a spear,
	Whan honted is the lyoun or the bere,	In the wild hunt of lion or of bear,
groves	And hereth him come ruschyng in the greves,	And heareth him come rushing through the wood,
breaking	And breketh bothe the bowes and the leves,	Crashing the branches in his madden'd mood,
	And thenketh, Here cometh my mortel enemy,	And think'th, "Here com'th my mortal enemy,
without	Withoute faile, he mot be deed or I;	Now without fail or he or I must die;
	For eyther I mot slen him at the gappe,	For either I must slay him at the gap,
	Or he moot slee me, if it me myshappe:	Or he must slay me if there be mishap."
their hue	So ferden they, in chaungyng of here hew,	So fared the knights so far as either knew,
far, them	As fer as eyther of hem other knewe.	When, seeing each, each deepen'd in his hue.
was not, saluting	Ther nas no good day, ne no saluyng;	There was no greeting—there was no 'Good day,'
	But streyt withouten wordes rehersyng,	But mute, without a single word, straightway
each, helped	Everich of hem helpeth to armen other,	Each one in arming turn'd to help the other,
own	As frendly, as he were his owen brother;	As like a friend as though he were his brother.
	And thanne with here scharpe speres stronge	And after that, with lances sharp and strong,
foined	They foyneden ech at other wonder longe,	They dash'd upon each other—lief and long.
then, seemed	Tho it semede that this Palamon	You might have fancied that this Palamon,
mad	In his fightyng were as a wood lyoun,	Fighting so blindly, were a mad lièn,
	And as a cruel tygre was Arcite:*	And like a cruel tiger was Arcite.
began	As wilde boores gonne they to smyte,	As two wild boars did they together smite,
their madness	That frothen white as fome, for ire wood,	That froth as white as foam for rage—they stood
their	Up to the ancle faught they in here blood.†	And fought until their feet were red with blood.
	And in this wise I lete hem fightyng dwelle;	Thus far awhile I leave them to their fight.
you	And forth I wol of Theseus yow telle.	And now what Theseus did I will recite.

Then something happened that neither of them expected.

It was a bright clear day, and Theseus, hunting with his fair queen Ipolita, and Emelye, clothed all in green, came riding by after the hart, with all the dogs around them; and as they followed the hart, suddenly Theseus looked out of the dazzle of the sun, and saw Arcite and Palamon in sharp fight, like two bulls for fury. The bright swords flashed to and fro so hideously that it seemed as though their smallest blows would fell an oak. But the duke knew not who they were that fought.‡

Theseus smote his spurs into his horse, and galloped in between the knights, and, drawing his sword,

---

* Even these similes separate the two characters: the lion may be mad with rage; the tiger, which is a cat, is crafty as well as fierce.

† An exaggeration simply for picturesque effect, such as many have indulged in since Chaucer.

‡ The helmet entirely concealing the face.

cried, "Ho!* No more, on pain of death! By mighty Mars, he dies who strikes a blow in my presence!" Then Theseus asked them what manner of men they were, who dared to fight there, without judge or witness, as though it were in royal lists?†

You may imagine the two men turning on Theseus, breathless and bloody with fight, weary with anger, and their vengeance still unslaked.

Glossary.		
	This Palamon answerde hastily,	And Palamon made answer hastily,
need	And seyde: Sire, what nedeth wordes mo?	And said—"O Sire, why should we waste more breath?
two	We han the deth deserved bothe tuo.	For both of us deserve to die the death.
wretches, captives	Tuo woful wrecches ben we, tuo kaytyves	Two wretched creatures are we, glad to die
encumbered by	That ben encombred of oure owne lyves,	Tired of our lives, tired of our misery—
	And as thou art a rightful lord and juge	And as thou art a rightful lord and judge
give us not	Ne yeve us neyther mercy ne refuge.	So give us neither mercy nor refuge!
holy	And sle me first, for seynte charite;	And slay me first, for holy charity—
also	But sle my felaw eek as wel as me.	But slay my fellow too as well as me!
little	Or sle him first; for, though thou know him lyte,	—Or slay him first, for though thou little know,
	This is thy mortal fo, this is Arcite,	This is Arcite—this is thy mortal foe,
	That fro thy lond is banyscht on his heed	Who from thy land was banished on his head,
deserved	For which he hath i-served to be deed.	For which he richly merits to be dead!
	For this is he that come to thi gate	Yea, this is he who came unto thy gate,
was named	And seyde, that he highte Philostrate.	And told thee that his name was Philostrate—
befooled	Thus hath he japed the ful many a yer,	Thus year by year hath he defied thine ire—
made	And thou hast maad of him thy cheef squyer.	And thou appointest him thy chiefest squire
	And this is he that loveth Emelye.	—And this is he who loveth Emelye!
	For sith the day is come that I schal dye,	"For since the day is come when I shall die,
	I make pleynly my confessioun,	Thus plain I make confession, and I own
that	That I am thilke woful Palamoun,	I am that miserable Palamon
wickedly	That hath thy prisoun broke wikkedly.	Who have thy prison broken wilfully!
	I am thy mortal foo, and it am I	I am thy mortal foe,—and it is I
	That loveth so hoote Emelye the brighte,	Who love so madly Emelye the bright,
	That I wol dye present in hire sighte.	That I would die this moment in her sight!
sentence	Therfore I aske deeth and my juwyse;	Therefore I ask death and my doom to-day—
slay	But slee my felaw in the same wyse,	But slay my fellow in the selfsame way:—
	For bothe we have served to be slayn.	For we have both deservëd to be slain."
	This worthy duk answerde anon agayn,	And angrily the duke replied again,
	And seyde: This is a schort conclusioun:	"There is no need to judge you any more,
own	Your owne mouth, by your confessioun,	Your own mouth, by confession, o'er and o'er
condemned	Hath dampned you bothe, and I wil it recorde.	Condemns you, and I will the words record.

* *Ho* was the word by which the heralds or the king commanded the cessation of any action.

† What were called the 'lists' were the places built and enclosed for combats on horseback, and tournaments. These combats got sometimes very serious, and many knights and horses were wounded, or even killed.

Glossary		
	It needeth nought to pyne yow with the corde. *	There is no need to pain you with the cord.
dead	Ye schul be deed by mighty Mars the reede!	Ye both shall die, by mighty Mars the red!"

Then the queen, 'for verray wommanhede,' began to weep, and so did Emelye, and all the ladies present. It seemed pitiful that two brave men, both of high lineage, should come to such an end, and only for loving a lady so faithfully. All the ladies prayed Theseus to have mercy on them, and pardon the knights for their sakes. They knelt at his feet, weeping and entreating him—

	And wold have kist his feet ther as he stood,	And would have kissed his feet there as he stood,
	Till atte laste aslaked was his mood;	Until at last appeasëd was his mood,
runneth	For pite renneth sone in gentil herte,	For pity springeth soon in gentle heart.
shook	And though he first for ire quok and sterte,	And though he first for rage did quake and start,
	He hath considerd shortly in a clause	He hath considered briefly in the pause
	The trespas of hem bothe, and eek the cause:	The greatness of their crime, and, too, its cause;
their	And although that his ire hire gylt accusede,	And while his passion had their guilt accused,
them	Yet in his resoun he hem bothe excusede.	Yet now his calmer reason both excused.

Everybody had sympathy for those who were in love,† and Theseus' heart 'had compassion of women, for they wept ever in on' (continually).

So the kindly duke softened, and said to all the crowd good-humouredly, "What a mighty and great lord is the god of love!"

here	Lo, her this Arcite and this Palamoun,	"Here are this Arcite and this Palamon,
freely (quit)	That quytely weren out of my prisoun,	Safe out of prison both, who might have gone
royally	And might have lyved in Thebes ryally,	And dwelt in Thebes city royally,
know, their	And witen I am here mortal enemy,	Knowing I am their mortal enemy,
their, lieth	And that here deth lith in my might also,	And that their death within my power lies:
	And yet hath love, maugré here eyghen tuo,	Yet hath blind Love, in spite of both their eyes,

* A form of torture to extort confession. Theseus' grim humour at this juncture implies how far lightlier human life was held then than now. But he was naturally in a great rage when he knew who the knights were. Palamon's insolent address in the *singular* personal pronoun was not likely to mollify him, coming as it did from a captive, though an equal by birth.

† How idealized, and how idolized, the passion of love had grown to be with the new elevation of woman's condition in these times is well known. Love literally covered a multitude of sins: the malefactor was pardoned whose offences were caused by love; the rough was made smooth for the feet of love to tread upon. There was a reason for this. It is but too true that the morals of the people will not bear the light of modern times; but it would be unfair to judge them by that light. Those were rough days, when laws were often feeble, narrow, or ill-enforced. The want of legal organization placed a great refining and ennobling power in the hands of woman. Many a knight, who was coarse or cowardly, was pricked to courteous ways and deeds of courage by his love of some fair woman, when without it he would have sunk lower and lower in vice and degradation. The arts were ofttimes cultivated to win a woman's ear or eye; knowledge itself was sought for her sake, for knowledge is power. Of course the love of courtesy, valour, and learning were deeply rooted in the age, or the woman's sympathy could not have existed. But her encouragement of all that was æsthetic, her influence over men, and therefore the impetus she gave to the higher life, must never be underrated, however we may reprove the errors of that day. The institution of actual 'Courts of Love'—tribunals for the judgment of love-matters, bearing a definite recognition, and which seem so strange, almost repulsive to us, presided over as they were by ladies only—was the result of the worship of physical beauty and the passion which it inspired, and the proof, however grotesque, of the real value seen to lie in it. This will be better understood when we observe that even children were encouraged to cultivate somewhat of this ideal love, and the childish education of boys and girls consisted to a very large extent in learning the art of writing love-letters. Thus Palamon's and Arcite's adoration of fresh Emelye are seen to be neither exaggerated nor futile.

Glossary		
	I-brought hem hider bothe for to dye.	Led them both hither only to be slain!
look, high	Now loketh, is nat that an heih folye?	Behold the height of foolishness most plain!
be	Who may not ben a fole, if that he love?	Who is so great a fool as one in love?
	Byholde for Goddes sake that sitteth above,	For mercy's sake—by all the gods above,
	Se how they blede! be they nought wel arrayed!	See how they bleed! a pretty pair are they!
them	Thus hath here lord, the god of love, hem payed	Thus their liege lord, the god of love, doth pay
their	Here wages and here fees for here servise.	Their wages, and their fees for service done;
think	And yet they wenen for to ben ful wise,	And yet each thinks himself a wise man's son
serve	That serven love, for ought that may bifalle.	Who serveth Love, whatever may befall.
	But this is yette the beste game of alle,	But this is still the greatest joke of all,
fun	That sche, for whom they have this jolitee,	That she, the cause of this rare jollity,
can them, much	Can hem therfore as moche thank as me.	Owes them about as many thanks as I!
knows	Sche woot no more of al this hoote fare,	She knew no more of all this hot to-do,
knows	By God, than wot a cuckow or an hare.	By Mars! than doth a hare or a cuckoo!
must be tried	But al moot ben assayed, hoot or colde;	But one must have one's fling, be't hot or cold;
must be, either	A man moot ben a fool other yong or olde;	A man will play the fool either young or old.
	I woot it by myself ful yore agon:	I know it by myself—for long ago
one	For in my tyme a servant was I on.	In my young days I bowed to Cupid's bow."

This is as if he should say, "These two foolish boys have got nothing from their liege lord, the god of love, but a very narrow escape with their heads. And Emelye herself knew no more of all this hot business than a cuckoo! But I, too, was young once, and in love, and so I won't be hard upon them!" "I will pardon you," he added, "for the queen's sake and Emelye's, but you must swear to me never to come and make war on me at any time, but be ever my friends in all that you may for the future."

And they were very thankful and promised as he commanded.

Then Theseus spoke again, in a kind, half laughing way:—

speak, royal	To speke of real lynage and riches,	"And as for wealth and rank, and royal birth,
princess	Though that sche were a quene or a prynces,	Although she were the noblest upon earth,
each	Ilk of yow bothe is worthy douteles	Each of you both deserves to wed your flame
marry, nevertheless	To wedden, when time is, but natheles	Being of equal worth; but all the same
	I speke as for my suster Emelye,	It must be said, my sister Emelye
	For whom ye have this stryf and jelousye,	(For whom ye have this strife and jealousy),
know	Ye woot yourself, sche may not wedde two	You see yourselves full well that she can never
once, fought	At oones, though ye faughten ever mo;	Wed two at once although ye fought for ever!
unwilling or willing	That oon of yow, or be him loth or leef,	But one of you, whether he likes or no,
must	He mot go pypen in an ivy leef;*	Must then go whistle, and endure his wo.
	This is to say, sche may nought now have bothe,	That is to say, she cannot have you both,
angry	Al be ye never so jelous, ne so wrothe.	Though you be never so jealous or so wroth."

* 'To pipe in an ivy leaf:' A proverbial expression, similar to 'go whistle'—meaning to be engaged in any useless employment.

With that he made them this offer—that Palamon and Arcite should each bring in a year's time (50 weeks) a hundred knights, armed for the lists,* and ready to do battle for Emelye; and whichever knight won, Palamon and his host or Arcite and his host, should have her for his wife.

Who looks happy now but Palamon? and who springs up with joy but Arcite! Every one was so delighted with the kindness of Theseus that they all went down on their knees to thank him—but of course Palamon and Arcite went on their knees most.

Now, would you like to know all the preparations Theseus made for this great tournament?

First, the theatre for the lists had to be built, where the tournament was to take place. This was built round in the form of a compass, with hundreds of seats rising up on all sides one behind another, so that everybody could see the fight, and no one was in anybody's way. The walls were a mile round, and all of stone, with a ditch running along the outside. At the east and at the west stood two gates of white marble, and there was not a carver, or painter, or craftsman of any kind that Theseus did not employ to decorate the theatre. So that there never was such a splendid place built in all the earth before or since.

Then he made three temples: one over the east gate for Venus, goddess of love; one over the west gate for Mars, who is god of war; and towards the north, he built a temple all of alabaster and red coral; and that was for Diana. All these beautiful things cost more money than would fill a big carriage.

Now I will tell you what the temples were like inside.

First, in the Temple of Venus were wonderful paintings of feasts, dancing, and playing of music, and beautiful gardens, and mountains, and people walking about with the ladies they liked. All these were painted on the walls in rich colour.

There was a statue of Venus besides, floating on a sea of glass, and the glass was made like waves that came over her. She had a citole in her hand, which is an instrument for playing music on; and over her head doves were flying. Little Cupid was also there, with his wings, and his bow and arrows, and his eyes blinded, as he is generally made.

Then, in the Temple of Mars, who is the god of war, there were all sorts of dangers and misfortunes painted. Battles, and smoke, and forests all burning with flames, and men run over by carts, and sinking ships, and many other awful sights. Then a smith forging iron—swords and knives for war.

The statue of Mars was standing on a car, armed and looking as grim as possible: there was a hungry wolf beside him.

As for the Temple of Diana, that was very different from Venus's. Venus wishes everybody to marry the one they love. Diana does not want any one to marry at all, but to hunt all day in the fields. So the pictures in Diana's Temple were all about hunting, and the merry life in the forest.

Her statue showed her riding on a stag, with dogs running round about, and underneath her feet was the moon. She was dressed in the brightest green, and she had a bow and arrows in her hand.

Now you know all about the splendid theatre and the three temples.

At last the day of the great tournament approached!

---

* The tournament, great as the loss of life often was, seems to have been the greatest delight of the people in the middle ages. The ladies especially loved them, as they were often in homage to themselves. The victor in the mimic battle received a crown from the queen of the tournament. In this case, Emelye is not asked whether she likes to be disposed of thus coolly! but she could not fail to be touched by the great compliment paid her.

Palamon and Arcite came to Athens as they had promised, each bringing with him a hundred knights, well armed; and never before, since the world began, was seen a sight so magnificent. Everybody who could bear arms was only too anxious to be among the two hundred knights—and proud indeed were those who were chosen! for you know, that if to-morrow there should be a like famous occasion, every man in England or anywhere else, who had a fair lady-love, would try to be there.

All the knights that flocked to the tournament wore shining armour according to their fancy. Some wore a coat of mail, which is chain-armour, and a breast-plate, and a gipon: others wore plate-armour, made of broad sheets of steel; some carried shields, some round targets. Again, some took most care of their legs, and carried an axe; others bore maces of steel.

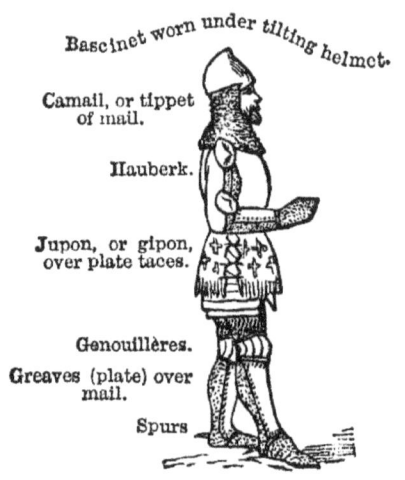 

It was on a Sunday, about nine o'clock in the morning, when all the lords and knights came into Athens.

With Palamon came the great Licurgus, King of Thrace; with Arcite came the mighty King of India, Emetrius: and I must give you the exact account of how these two kings looked, which is most minute. I should not wonder if these were the likenesses of Palamon and Arcite themselves. *

First, then, comes—

Glossary		
	Ligurge himself, the grete kyng of Trace;	Licurge himself, the mighty king of Thrace;
	Blak was his berd, and manly was his face.	Black was his beard, and manly was his face,
eyes	The cercles of his eyen in his heed	The circles of his eyes within his head
between	They gloweden bytwixe yolw and reed,	Glow'd of a hue part yellow and part red,
	And lik a griffoun loked he aboute,	And like a griffon lookëd he about,
stout	With kempe heres † on his browes stowte;	With hair down-combed upon his brows so stout;

* There are no portraits, otherwise, of these two princes, whose characters are so clear and forcible all through that some physical description is sorely needed. The portraits of the two sovereigns fit singularly well the fierce, passionate nature of Palamon, and the cooler but equally noble one of Arcite.

† *Kemped heres*: Dr. Morris rejects the usual rendering of the word kemped as combed, and asserts that it means the very reverse, and, "instead of smoothly combed, means bent, *curled*, and hence rough, shaggy." A similar term occurs a few lines farther on, describing the hair 'kempt behind his back,' where Dr. Morris reads combed. It seems, however, contrary to the rule of courtesy observed by lovers, that a noble knight should appear at a festival like a wild man of the woods. If, on the other hand, the shaggy hairs were on the *eyebrow*, it certainly adds to the ferocity of his look. I prefer the former reading for Emelye's bridegroom.

limbs, muscles	His lymes grete, his brawnes hard and stronge,	His limbs were great, his muscles hard and strong,
shoulders	His schuldres brood, his armes rounde and longe.	His shoulders broad, his arms were round and long.
guise	And as the gyse was in his contre,	According to the fashion of his land,
high, car	Ful heye upon a chare of gold stood he,	Full high upon a car of gold stood he,
bulls, the traces	With foure white boles in a trays.	And to the car four bulls were link'd, milk-white.
	In stede of cote armour on his harnays, *	'Stead of coat-armour on his harness bright,
	With nales yolwe, and bright as eny gold,	With yellow nails and bright as any gold,
very old	He had a bere skyn, cole-blak for-old.	A bear's skin hung, coal-black, and very old.
long hair combed	His lange heer y-kempt byhynd his bak,	His flowing hair was comb'd behind his back,
shone	As eny raven fether it schon for blak.	As any raven's wing it shone for black.
	A wrethe of gold arm-gret, and huge of wighte,	A wreath of gold, arm-thick, of monstrous weight,
	Upon his heed, set ful of stoones brighte,	Crusted with gems, upon his head was set,
diamonds	Of fyne rubies and of fyn dyamauntz.	Full of fine rubies and clear diamonds.
	Aboute his chare ther wenten white alauntz,†	About his car there leapèd huge white hounds,
steer (bullock)	Twenty and mo, as grete as eny stere,	Twenty and more, as big as any steer,
	To hunt at the lyoun or at the bere,	To chase the lion or to hunt the bear,
muzzle	And folwed him, with mosel fast i-bounde,	And follow'd him, with muzzles firmly bound,
spikes, filled	Colerd with golde, and torettz ‡ fyled rounde.	Collar'd in gold, with golden spikes around.

The other portrait has a less barbaric splendour about it.

India	The gret Emetreus, the kyng of Ynde,	The great Emetrius, the Indian King,
	Uppon a steede bay, trapped in steel,	Upon a bay steed trapp'd in shining steel,
diapered	Covered with cloth of gold dyapred wel,	Covered with cloth of gold from head to heel,
like	Cam rydyng lyk the god of armes, Mars.	Came riding like the god of armies, Mars;
	His coote armour was of a cloth of Tars, §	His coat-armour was made of cloth of Tars,
overlaid	Cowched of perlys whyte, round and grete.	O'erlaid with pearls all white and round and great:
burnished	His sadil was of brend gold new i-bete;	His saddle was of smooth gold, newly beat.
mantle	A mantelet ‖ upon his schuldre hangyng	A mantlet on his shoulder as he came,
cram-full, fire	Bret-ful of rubies reed, as fir sparclyng.	Shone, cramm'd with rubies sparkling like red flame,
run	His crispe her lik rynges was i-ronne,	And his crisp hair in shining rings did run,

* See page 42, note.

† *Alauns.* A species of dog used for hunting the boar, &c. Sp. *alano.* Speght says they were greyhounds, Tyrwhitt mastiffs, much esteemed in Italy in the 14th century. See Cotgrave—'*Allan,* a kind of big, strong, thick-headed, and short-snowted dog—the brood whereof came first out of Albania.'

‡ See Appendix, p. 111.   § A kind of rich silk.

‖ The 'mantelet' was at first devised to protect the burnished helmet from becoming inconveniently heated by the sun: it became afterwards fantastic in form, and is the origin of the 'mantling' seen in modern coats of arms.

Glossary		
yellow-brown	And that was yalwe, and glityryng as the sonne.	Yellow it was, and glittering as the sun.
	His nose was heigh, his eyen bright cytryn,	His nose was high, his eyes were bright citrine,
	His lippes rounde, his colour was sangwyn,	His lips were round, his colour was sanguine,
sprinkled	A fewe freknes in his face y-spreynd,	With a few freckles scattered here and there,
somewhat, mixed	Betwixe yolwe and somdel blak y-meynd,	'Twixt black and yellow mingling they were,
looking	And as a lyoun he his lokyng caste.	And lion-like his glance went to and fro.
suppose	Of fyve and twenty yeer his age I caste.	His age was five and twenty years, I trow.
	His berd was wel bygonne for to sprynge;	A downy beard had just begun to spring,
	His voys was as a trumpe thunderynge.	His voice was like a trumpet thundering.
laurel	Upon his heed he wered of laurer grene	Upon his head he wore a garland green,
	A garlond freische and lusty for to sene.	Of laurel, fresh, and pleasant to be seen.
hand, delight	Upon his hond he bar for his deduyt *	Upon his wrist he bore for his delight
eagle, any	An egle tame, as eny lylie whyt.	An eagle, tame, and as a lily white.

There was a great festival, and the dancing, and minstrelsy, and feasting, and rich array of Theseus' palace were most wondrous to behold. I should never have time to tell you

be	What ladies fayrest ben, or best daunsynge,	What ladies danced the best, or fairest were,
sing	Or which of hem can carole † best and singe,	Or which of them best sung or carol'd there;
	Ne who most felyngly speketh of love;	Nor who did speak most feelingly of love,
sit	What haukes sitten on the perche above,	What hawks were sitting on the perch above,
lie	What houndes liggen on the floor adoun.	What hounds lay crouching on the floor adown.

Then there were the temples to visit, to ask grace and favour from the gods. Palamon went to the Temple of Venus, the goddess of love, and prayed her to help him to gain his lady. Venus promised him success.

Arcite thought it more prudent to go to the god of war, Mars; so he sacrificed in his temple, and prayed for victory in the lists. Mars promised him the victory.

But Emelye did not wish to marry either of her lovers. She went to the temple of Diana early in the morning, and asked the goddess to help her not to get married! She preferred her free life, walking in the woods and hunting. She made two fires on Diana's altar: but Diana would not listen to her, and both the fires went out suddenly, with a whistling noise, and Emelye was so frightened that she began to cry. Then Diana told her she was destined to marry one of these poor knights who had suffered so much for her, and so she must make up her mind to it.

* This fair countenance is oddly assigned to an Indian monarch: but some of the details of his appearance are poetic embellishments and must not be relied upon. The white eagle carried for his pleasure is probably one of the many exaggerations for picturesque effect, and is only a magnified falcon, a bird which was at this time the constant companion of the noble: hawking was in high favour, and the bird's tameness depended on its habituation to its owner's voice and touch. A little later on the hawks are mentioned as sitting on perches during the festival; such perches were in every room and hall in common life; so provision had to be made for their accommodation on the grandest occasions. In Wright's 'Womankind,' we read: "Different species of the hawk were allotted to persons of the different grades and ranks of society. Thus we are told that the eagle and the vulture belonged to the emperor, from which we must understand that the emperor was not expected to go often a-hawking." Evidently Chaucer was well read in his books on falconry.

† *Carole* (Tyrwhitt—the other editions have *dance*) was a round dance.

THE KNIGHT'S TALE

Emelye then departed: but Mars and Venus had a great dispute, because, as you know, they had promised success to each of the two knights, and Emelye could not marry both. Now, you shall see how each of them managed to gain a victory.

All Monday was spent in jousting and dancing, and early on Tuesday began the great tourney.

Such a stamping of horses and chinking of harness!* Such lines and crowds of horsemen! There you might see armour so rare and so rich, wrought with goldsmith's work, and embroidery, and steel! Helmets and hauberks and trappings—squires nailing on the spearheads, and buckling helmets—rubbing up the shields, and lacing the plates with thongs of leather. Nobody was idle.

GLOSSARY.

The fomy stedes on the golden bridel	The foamy steeds upon the golden bridle
Gnawyng, and faste the armurers also	Gnawing, and fast the armourers also
With fyle and hamer prikyng to and fro;	With file and hammer pricking to and fro;
Yemen on foote, and communes many oon	Yeomen on foot, and flocking thro' the land
With schorte staves, thikke as they may goon.	Commons with short staves, thick as they can stand.

commons } many a one go

Pipes, trumpets, drums, and clarions were heard, that serve to drown the noise of battle with music—little groups of people gathered about the palace, here three—there ten—arguing the merits of the two Theban knights. Some said one thing, some another. Some backed the knight with the black beard, others the bald one, others the knight with close hair. Some said, "*He* looks grim, and will fight!" and "*He* hath an axe that weighs twenty pound!"

Duke Theseus sits at a window, like a god on his throne. The masses of people are pressing towards him to see him, and to salute him humbly, and to hear his commands, and his decree!

A herald on a tall scaffold shouts out *"Ho!"* till all the noise of the people is hushed, and when all is quiet, he tells them the duke's will:—

"My lord hath of his wisdom considered that it were destruction to gentle blood to fight in this tourney, as in mortal battle. Therefore, to save life, he now changes his first purpose.

"No arrows, pole-axe, or short knife shall be brought into the lists, no short sword, either in the hand or worn at the side. No man shall ride more than one course with a sharp spear. Whoso comes to harm shall be taken, and not slain, but brought to the stake, there to abide according to order. And should a chieftain on either side be taken, or slay his fellow, no longer shall the tourney last. God speed you, go forth, and lay on fast! Fight your fill with mace and longsword!" †

The shouts of all the people rang right up to the sky, "God save such a good lord, who will have no bloodshed!"

Up go the trumpets and the music, and through the broad city, all hung with cloth of gold, the crowds ride to the lists. The noble duke rode first, and the Theban knights on either side, afterwards came the queen and fair Emelye, and then all the company followed according to their rank.

When they came to the lists, everybody pressed forward to the seats. Arcite goes in at the west gate by Mars' temple, with a red banner, and all his hundred knights. At the same moment Palamon enters the east gate by Venus' temple, with his white banner and brave host. Never was there such a

---

* The term for the whole panoply of knight or steed—armour and coat-armour included.

† A knight in armour was in very little danger from a cut of a broadsword, or even from the blow of a mace; but a thrusting sword might easily pierce through the joints of his armour.—*Bell*.

sight. The two companies were so evenly matched there was no choosing between them. Then they ranged themselves in two ranks; the names were read out, that there might be no cheating in the numbers; the gates were shut, and loud was the cry, "Do now your devoir, young knights proud!"

The heralds have ceased to ride up and down. The trumpets ring out—in go the spears steadily to the rests—the sharp spur is in the horse's side. There you may see who can joust and who can ride—there the shafts of the spears shiver on the thick shields—he feels the thrust right through the body. Up spring the lances twenty foot high, out fly the swords like silver—helmets are crushed and shivered—out bursts the blood in stern, red streams! See, the strong horses stumble—down go all—a man rolls under foot like a ball. See, he fences at his foe with a truncheon, and hustles him while his horse is down. He is hurt through the body, and is dragged off to the stake—and there he must stay. Another is led off to that other side. All the humane orders of Theseus are forgotten.

From time to time Theseus stops the fray to give time for refreshment and drink, should the combatants need it.

Often have these two Thebans fought before now; each has often unhorsed the other. But in spite of Theseus' commands, never was tiger bereft of its young so cruel in the hunt, as Arcite in his jealousy was on Palamon. Never was hunted lion, mad with hunger, so eager for blood as Palamon for Arcite's life. See, they are both bleeding.

As the day went by, many in the field were carried away by excitement. The strong King Emetrius flew at Palamon as he fought with Arcite, and ran his sword into him. Then there was a frightful uproar. Emetrius could not govern himself, and was dragged off to the stake by the force of twenty men, and while trying to rescue Palamon, the great King Licurge was borne down; and King Emetrius, despite his strength, was flung out of his saddle a sword's length, so violently Palamon hit at him; but he was carried to the stake for all that, and this tumult put an end to the tourney, according to the rule Theseus had made.

How bitterly wretched was Palamon, now that he could not ride any more at his foe! Only by an unfair attack had he lost ground. Theseus, seeing them all fighting together wildly, cried out *"Ho!"* and stopped the tourney. Then he said, "I will be a true judge, and impartial. Arcite of Thebes shall have Emelye, who, by good luck, has fairly won her!"

Shouts of delight answered Theseus, till it seemed as if the theatre would fall with the noise.

It is said that Venus was so disappointed at Palamon, her knight, losing, that she wept, and went for help to her father, the god Saturn. Saturn said to her, "Daughter, hold thy peace; Mars has had his way, but you shall yet have yours!"

Now you shall see what happened.

This fierce Arcite, hearing the duke's decision, and the cries and yells of the heralds and all the people, raised his visor and spurred his horse along the great place and looked up at Emelye. And Emelye looked down at him kindly (for women always follow the favour of fortune), and smiled.

It was in this sweet moment, when he was off his guard, that something startled his tired and excited horse, and it leapt aside and foundered as it leapt, and before Arcite could save himself, he was flung down, and his breast-bone smashed against the saddle-bow—so that he lay as dead, his face black with the sudden rush of blood.

Poor Arcite! to lose all, just in the moment of supreme joy and victory!

He was carried out of the lists, broken-hearted, to Theseus' palace, where his harness was cut off him, and he was laid in a beautiful bed. He was still conscious, and always asking piteously for Emelye.

As for Duke Theseus, he came back to the town of Athens in great state and cheer. Were it not for this unlucky accident at the end, there had not been a single mishap, and as the leeches said Arcite would soon be well again, *that* was no such great disaster. None had been actually killed, though many had been grievously wounded: which was very gratifying. For all the broken arms could be mended, and the bruises and cuts healed with salves and herbs and charms.

There had even been no discomfiture, for falls did not count as shame, nor was it any disgrace to be dragged to a stake with kicks and hootings, and held there hand and foot all alone, whilst one's horse was driven out by the sticks of the grooms. That was no disgrace, for it was not cowardice; and such things *must* happen at a tourney. And so all the people made mirth.

The duke gave beautiful gifts to all the foreign knights, and there were ever so many more shows and feasts for the next three days, and the two mighty kings had the greatest honour paid them, till all men had gone home to their houses.

So there was an end of the great battle.

But Arcite did not get well so soon as they thought he would. His wound swelled up, and the sore increased at his heart more and more. He was so injured that the balms and the salves gave him no ease, and nature could not do her part. And when nature cannot work, farewell physic! there is no more to be done but carry the man to the churchyard.

In short, Arcite was evidently dying, and he sent for Emelye, who held herself his wife, and for Palamon, his cousin, and they both came to his bedside.

Then he told Emelye all the sorrow that was in his heart, at losing her whom he had loved so dearly; and how he still loved her, and wanted her to pray for him when he was dead.

GLOSSARY.

pains	Allas, the woo! allas, the peynes stronge	"Alas, the woe! alas, the trials strong
suffered	That I for you have suffred, and so longe!	That I for you have borne—and, ah, so long!
death	Allas, the deth! allas, myn Emelye!	Alas, to die! alas, mine Emelye!
separating	Allas, departyng of our compainye!	Alas, that we so soon part company!
	Allas, myn hertes queen! allas, my wyf!	Alas, my heart's one queen! alas, my wife!
	Myn hertes lady, endere of my lyf!	Ah, my heart's lady, ender of my life!
ask	What is this world? what asken men to have?	What is life worth? what do men yearn to have?
	Now with his love, now in his colde grave	Now with his darling—now in his cold grave,
any	Allone, withouten eny compainye!	Alone, alone, and with no company!
foe	Farwel, my swete foo! myn Emelye! *	Farewell, my sweet foe—farewell, Emelye,
two	And softe tak me in youre armes tweye,	And softly take me in your arms to-day
hearken	For love of God, and herkneth what I seye.	For love of God, and listen what I say."

Then Arcite pointed to Palamon, and said—

I have heer with my cosyn Palamon   "I have here with my cousin Palamon

---

* Tyrwhitt's and Bell's editions read, 'Farwel, my swete, farwel, myn Emelye!'

| Glossary. | Had stryf and rancour many a day agon | Had strife and hatred days and years agone |
| | For love of yow, and for my jelousie. | For love of you, and for my jealousy. |

. . . .

	So Jupiter have of my soule part,	So Jupiter have of my soul a part,
	As in this world right now ne knowe I non	As in the whole wide world now know I none
	So worthy to be loved as Palamon,	So worthy to be loved as Palamon,
	That serveth you, and wol don al his lyf.	Who served you well, and will do all his life.
shall	And if that evere ye schul ben a wyf,	Therefore, if ever you shall be a wife,
forget	Foryet not Palamon, the gentil man.	Forget not Palamon, that noble man."

began to fail	And with that word his speche faille gan,	And with that word his speech to fail began,
	For fro his feete up to his brest was come	For from his feet up to his breast was come
	The cold of deth, that hadde him overnome.*	The cold of death, that hath him overcome.
already	And yet moreover in his armes two	And now moreover, in his arms at last
gone	The vital strengthe is lost, and al ago.	The vital strength is lost, and all is past.
without	Only the intellect, withouten more,	Only the intellect, all clear before,
	That dwellede in his herte sik and sore,	That lingered in his heart so sick and sore,
began to fail	Gan fayllen, when the herte felte deth;	Began to falter when the heart felt death,
darkened, failed }	Dusked his eyen two, and failled his breth.	Then his two eyes grew dark, and faint his breath,
	But on his lady yit caste he his eye;	But on his lady yet cast he his eye;
	His laste word was—*Mercy, Emelye.*	And his last word was—*"Mercy, Emelye."*

He was dead.

Emelye was carried away from Arcite, fainting; and the sorrow she felt is more than I can tell. Day and night she wept, for she had learned to love Arcite as much as if he had been already her husband, so that she was nigh to dying.

All the city mourned for him, young and old. Theseus, and Palamon, and everybody was filled with grief. Never had there been such sorrow.

Theseus had a splendid bier made, for Arcite to be burned according to the custom, with the greatest honours. Huge oak trees were cut down on purpose to burn on his pile. Arcite's body was covered with cloth of gold, with white gloves on his hands, his sword by his side, and a wreath of laurel on his head. His face was uncovered, so that all the people might see him, when he was carried forth from the great hall of the palace.

Theseus ordered that Arcite should be burned in that very grove where Palamon and Arcite had first fought for love of Emelye, on that sweet May morning a year ago. So the funeral pile was raised in that grove.

Three beautiful white horses, covered with glittering steel harness and the arms of Arcite, bore all his armour and weapons before him to the spot.

---

* Tyrwhitt. *Overnome* is participle past of *overnimen* (Sax.), to overtake. The following, and the sixth line further on, are also Tyrwhitt's reading.

The whole city was hung with black, and the noblest Greeks in the land carried the bier. Duke Theseus, and his old father Egeus, and Palamon, walked beside it, carrying in their hands golden cups, full of milk and wine and blood, to throw upon the pile. Then came Emelye, weeping, with fire in her hand, as the custom was, wherewith to set light to the pile.

With great care and ceremony the wood and straw were built up around the body, so high that they seemed to reach to the sky, and cloth of gold and garlands of flowers were hung all round it.

Poor Emelye fainted when she set fire to the pile, in the course of the funeral service, for her grief was more than she could bear. As soon as the fire burned fast, perfumes and jewels were flung in, and Arcite's shield, spear, and vestments, and the golden cups. Then all the Greeks rode round the fire to the left, three times shouting, and three times rattling their spears; and three times the women cried aloud.

And when all was over, Emelye was led home; and there were curious ceremonies performed, called the lykewake, at nightfall.

Long afterwards, Theseus sent for Palamon. The mourning for Arcite was over in the city, but Palamon came, still wearing his black clothes, quite sorrowful.

Then Theseus brought Emelye to Palamon, and reminded them both of Arcite's dying words. He took Emelye's hand and placed it in the hand of Palamon. Then Palamon and Emelye were married, and they lived happy ever after.

G<small>LOSSARY</small>.

welfare	For now is Palamon in alle wele,	For now this Palamon hath all the wealth,
health	Lyvynge in blisse, in richesse, and in hele;	Living in bliss, in riches, and in health;
	And Emelye him loveth so tendrely,	And Emelye loveth him so tenderly,
nobly	And he hire serveth al so gentilly,	And he doth cherish her so faithfully,
there, between	That nevere was ther no word hem bitweene	That all their days no thought they had again
affliction	Of jelousye, or any other teene.	Of jealousy, nor any other pain.
	Thus endeth Palamon and Emelye,	Thus endeth Palamon and Emelye,
fair	And God save al this fayre compainye.	And God save all this kindly company!

Notes by the Way.

T<small>HE</small> outline of the foregoing Tale was borrowed by Chaucer from Boccaccio's 'Theseida:' but the treatment and conception of character are wholly his own.

It is a common thing to say of the Knight's Tale that with all its merits the two principal actors, Arcite and Palamon, are very much alike, and constantly may be mistaken for each other. It seems to me that to say such a thing is a proof of not having read the tale, for the characters of the two men are almost diametrically opposed, and never does one act or speak as the other would do.

Notice, therefore, the striking contrast all through the story between the characters. From the first, Arcite in the prison is seen to be cooler and more matter-of-fact than Palamon, whose violent nature suffers earliest from imprisonment, mentally, perhaps morally; and whom we find pacing restlessly about, and ceaselessly bemoaning his fate, while Arcite is probably sitting still in philosophic resignation.

Palamon is clearly a man of violent, uncontrolled passions—reckless, even rash, and frantically jealous. Arcite's is by far the stronger mind—wise, clever, cool, but quite as brave and fervent as his friend. Every incident brings out their character in strong relief. To Palamon it is given to see Emelye first. He mistakes her for Venus, and prays to her as such—his mind being probably slightly disordered by the privations of mediæval prison life, as a mind so excitable would soon become. Arcite recognizes her instantly as a woman, and claims her calmly. Palamon 'flies out,' reproaches him bitterly, violently, with the term most abhorrent to the chivalrous spirit of the time—'false.' Arcite answers with passion, but he is matter-of-fact in the midst of it, reminding his friend how little consequence it is to either of them, for both are perpetual prisoners; and he can even wind up with a touch of humour, quoting the two fighting dogs and the kite.

On his release from prison, Arcite follows out successfully a most difficult *rôle*, concealing his identity in the midst of Theseus' court, and in the agitating presence of his lady, at the risk of his life—*for years:* a stratagem requiring constant *sang-froid* and self-control, which would have been as impossible to Palamon, as mistaking a beautiful woman for a divine vision would have been to Arcite. He does not forget Palamon during this time, though powerless to help him. He is unselfish enough to pray Juno for him, in his soliloquy in the wood.

At the meeting of the rivals in the wood, Palamon, mastered at once by rage, bids Arcite fight with him, that instant, regardless of his (Palamon's) being unarmed: he fears nothing, he only wants to fight. Arcite, also furious, can nevertheless see the common-sense side of the affair, and the need for fair play and proper accoutrements; and enumerates very sensibly the arms and other necessaries he will bring Palamon, including (so matter-of-fact is he) *food and bedding for the night*.

When the combatants are discovered in their illegal and unwitnessed fight, Palamon does not fear death. He is only anxious that, whether he be dead or alive, Arcite shall not have Emelye; and reiterates his entreaty that Arcite may be slain too—before or after, he doesn't care which, as long as he is slain.

Palamon's intense jealousy, which could face death cheerfully, but not the yielding up of his beloved to another man, and his anxiety that Arcite should not survive him, are of course less ignoble than they seem if viewed in the light of the times. It was this same jealousy which prompted him to betray Arcite as soon as he got the chance—forgetting that Arcite had not betrayed *him*, the day before, when he was in his power. But Chaucer himself once or twice refers to his mind being unhinged—'wood for love'—which claims our forbearance.

Again, the *appearance* of Licurge (taken as Palamon's portrait) is very characteristic. His eye is fierce, his get-up is mighty, barbaric, bizarre; but Emetrius (Arcite) appears in a much more usual way. Licurge mounts a chariot drawn by bulls—Emetrius rides on horseback, like an ordinary knight. Licurge is enveloped in a bear's hide—Emetrius is properly caparisoned.

It is also noteworthy that Palamon entreats *Venus* for success, for he can think of nothing but his love: Arcite thinks it more prudent to address *Mars*, since he has got to win Emelye by fight—he has *considered* the question, you see; and it is therefore (I think) that the preference is given to Palamon in marrying Emelye, because society so exalted the passion of love in those days, while Arcite is made to suffer for his very prudence, which *might* argue a less absorbing passion.

It was a master-thought to make Arcite die by an accident, so that neither of the rivals vanquished the other, and Palamon escapes the possible reproach of winning his happiness by slaying his friend.

The sympathy, however, remains with Arcite. His character is beautifully developed. It is not inconsistent with his power of self-control and brave heart, noble throughout, that he is able to make such a sacrifice on his death-bed as to give Emelye to Palamon. It is a sign of forgiveness of Palamon, who, at the point of death, showed no such generosity; and the greatness of the sacrifice must be estimated by remembering the mediæval view of love and love-matters.

I do not think that Palamon could have done that, any more than he could have concealed his identity in Theseus' court.*

* See *Chaucer for Schools*, p. 86, for some curious details.

The Friar's Tale.

THIS worthy Friar (Chaucer says), as he rode along with the rest of the company, kept looking askance at the Summoner, whom he evidently regarded as an enemy,* and though, as yet, for common civility's sake, he had not said anything to him which could cause a regular quarrel, it was quite plain there was little love lost between them.

When his turn came to tell his story, he saw a chance of annoying the Summoner, which he didn't mean to lose; and, disagreeable as the Summoner was, it is not very surprising.

G<small>LOSSARY</small>.

	But if it like to this companye,	"But if agreeable to the company,
joke	I wil yow of a Sompnour telle a game;	I'll tell you of a Summoner such a game!
	Pardé, ye may wel knowe by the name,	Belike you may imagine from the name,
	That of a Sompnour may no good be sayd;	That of a Summoner can no good be said.
disappointed	I pray that noon of yow be evel apayd.	I pray that none of you be ill repaid!"

The Summoner, who was inoffensive enough just then, whatever he might have been at other times, was not very well pleased at having his trade spoken of in such terms, and felt that it was all a hit at himself; and mine host, to prevent further squabbling, breaks in with—"Now, Friar, it is not very courteous to speak at a companion in that style; a man of your calling ought to know better:—

	In companye we wol have no debaat:	"In company we will have no debate,
tell	Telleth your tale, and let the Sompnour be.	Tell on your tale, and let the Summoner be."
	Nay, quoth the Sompnour, let him saye to me	"Nay," cried the Summoner, "let him say of me
	What so him list; whan it cometh to my lot	What he may choose. When my turn comes, good lack!

---

* The Summoners and the Friars were naturally always at variance, both deriving their money from the same Source: both belonged to the Church, but the Summoner was legally qualified to *extort*, whilst the Friar was only permitted to *beg*. Thus, if the Summoner had been to a house first, the Friar was likely to suffer.

GLOSSARY.		
requite, groat	By God I schal him quyten every grot.	All he has said I'll pay him fairly back!
great	I schal him telle which a gret honour	I'll tell him what a pretty trade is his,
be, false	Is to ben a fals flateryng lymytour!	Beggar and flattering limitor that he is!"

Mine host cries out, "Peace, no more of this!" and begs the Friar to go on.

ONCE upon a time there was an archdeacon in my country who punished with great severity all kinds of misdoings.

He had a Summoner ready to his hand, who worked under this strict archdeacon with equal severity. A slyer fellow was there none in England; and most cunningly he watched the people in secret, so as to find out how best to catch them tripping.

I shall not spare this Summoner here, though he be mad as a hare with it all; for Summoners have no jurisdiction over us Friars, you know, and never will have, all the days of their lives. We are out of their power!

["So are other refuse of the people* besides Friars!" interrupted the angry Summoner, when he heard that.

"Peace, with bad luck to you!" cries mine host, also getting angry; "and let the Friar tell his story. Now tell on, master, and let the Summoner gale!" †]

This false thief—this Summoner—used to find out, in all sorts of underhand ways, what people did, right or wrong, by spying in secret, and by keeping people to spy for him. And when he found out anybody doing wrong, he would threaten to summon them before the court, and they used to bribe him with money to let them off. If they were too poor to bribe him, he would make the archdeacon punish them; but if they had enough money to give him, he did not care how many bad things they did, and never told the archdeacon. This was very unjust and wicked, as it encouraged people to do wrong; and the Summoner grew quite rich in this evil way, for he kept all the money himself, and did not give it to the archdeacon. He was, you see, a thief as well as a spy;

	For in this world nys dogge for the bowe ‡	No dog on earth that's trainëd to the bow
whole	That can an hurt dere from an hol y-knowe,	Can a hurt deer from an unhurt one know,

better than this cunning man knew what everybody was about,—

because	And for that was the fruyt of al his rent,	And, since that was the source of all his pelf,
thereon, purpose	Therfore theron he set al his entent.	To winning gain he did devote himself.
befell, once	And so bifel, that oones on a day	And so it chanc'd that, once upon a day,
	This Sompnour, ever wayting on his pray,	This Summoner, ever waiting for his prey,

* Houses of ill-fame were exempted from ecclesiastical interference on the ground that they were a necessary evil, and might be thus better *surveillé*.

† *Gale*—sing: it means here, 'If the Summoner likes to squeak when he feels the shoe pinch, let him!'

‡ "A dog trained for shooting with the bow, part of whose education consisted in following the stricken deer only, and separating it from the herd."—*Bell*.

GLOSSARY.	Rod forth to sompne a widew, an old ribibe,*	Rode forth to summon a widow, a poor soul,
	Feynyng a cause, for he wolde han a bribe.	And feign'd a cause, that he might get a dole.
saw	And happede that he say bifore him ryde	It happen'd that he saw before him ride
	A gay yeman under a forest syde.	A yeoman gay, along the forest side.
	A bowe he bar, and arwes bright and kene;	A bow he bore, and arrows, bright and keen;
short cloak	He had upon a courtepy of grene;	He had on a short upper cloak of green;
head	An hat upon his heed with frenges blake.	A black-fringed hat upon his head was set.
overtaken	Sir, quoth this Sompnour, heyl and wel overtake.	The Summoner cried out, "Hail, sir, and well met!"
fellow	Welcome, quod he, and every good felawe.	"Welcome," quoth he, "and every one as good!
ridest thou, wood	Whider ridestow under this grene schawe?	And whither ridest thou in this green wood?
	(Sayde this yiman) wiltow fer to-day?	(The yeoman said) and is it far you go?"
	This Sompnour him † answerd and sayde, Nay:	The Summoner made answer, and said, "No:
purpose	Here faste by, quod he, is myn entent	Close handy here my errand lies," quoth he,
raise	To ryden, for to reysen up a rent	"I ride to raise a rent that's owing me,
duty	That longith to my lordes dueté.	Belonging to my master's property."

"Art thou a bailiff, then?" asks the yeoman. The Summoner was ashamed to say what he really was, so he said, "Yes."

"Good," said the stranger. "Thou art a bailiff and I am another. Let us be friends. I am unknown in this country; but if you will come and see me in my country, I have plenty of gold and silver in my chest, and I will share it all with you."

"Thank you," said the greedy Summoner; and they shook hands, and promised to be staunch friends and sworn brothers till they died! And thus they rode on together.

The Summoner, who was always inquisitive and asking questions, was very anxious to know where he could find this amiable new friend, who was so free with his money.

	Brother, quoth he, wher now is your dwellyng,	"Brother," quoth he, "your dwelling now, where is't,
seek	Another day if that I schulde yow seeche?	If I some future day the place could reach?"

Notice the cunning yeoman's answer:—

	This yiman him answered in softe speche:	The yeoman answered him in softest speech:
	Brother, quod he, fer in the north ‡ contre,	"Brother," quoth he, "far in the north countree,
where	Wheras I hope somtyme I schal the se;	Whereat I hope sometime I shall thee see.
separate, teach	Er we depart I schal the so wel wisse,	Before we part I shall direct thee so,
shalt thou, miss	That of myn hous ne schaltow never misse.	Thou canst not fail my dwelling-place to know."

* *Ribibe:* a shrill musical instrument—metaphorical for a shrill old woman.

† Tyrwhitt.

‡ The hell of the Teutonic race, before they were Christians, was in the north, and after their conversion, as their converters adopted their name, only giving the place a Christian character, it was natural that the people should retain their original notion of its position.—*Bell.*

You will see later why he was so anxious to bring the Summoner to his own dwelling.

GLOSSARY.

you	Now, brother, quod this Sompnour, I yow pray	"Now, brother," said the Summoner, "I pray,
ride	Teche me, whil that we ryden by the way,	Teach me while we are riding on our way,
since, be	Syn that ye ben a baily as am I,	Since you a bailiff are, as well as I,
subtilty	Som subtilte, as tel me faithfully	Some subtle craft, and tell me faithfully
my	In myn office how I may moste * wynne.	How in my office I most gold may win,
refrain	And spare not for consciens or for synne,	And hide not aught for conscience or for sin,
	But, as my brother, tel me how do ye?	But as my brother, tell me how do ye?"

The strange yeoman is delighted at these questions, and you will see that in his answer he pretends to describe himself, but he is really describing all the Summoner does!

	Now, by my trouthe, brothir myn, sayde he,	"Now, by my troth, my brother dear," quoth he,
	As I schal telle the a faithful tale.	"I will be frank with you, and tell you all:
narrow, small	My wages ben ful streyt and eek ful smale;	The wages that I get are very small,
severe	My lord to me is hard and daungerous,	My master's harsh to me, and stingy too,
laborious	And myn office is ful laborous,	And hard is all the work I have to do;
	And therfor by extorciouns † I lyve.	And therefore by extortion do I live.
give	Forsoth I take al that men wil me yive,	Forsooth, I take what any one will give;
always, cunning	Algate by sleighte or by violence,	Either by cunning or by violence
	Fro yer to yer I wynne my despence,	From year to year I snatch my year's expense.
	I can no better telle faithfully.	No better can I tell you honestly."
	Now, certes, quod this Sompnour, so fare I.	"Now, truly," cried the Summoner, "so do I!
knows	I spare not to take, God it woot,	I never spare to take a thing, God wot,
unless	But-if it be to hevy or to hoot. ‡	Unless it be too heavy or too hot.
get	What I may gete in counseil prively,	What I can grasp by counsel privily,
conscience	No more consciens of that have I;	No scruples in that matter trouble me.
were it not for	Nere myn extorcions I mighte not lyven,	Without extortion I could ne'er subsist,
games, shriven	Ne of such japes I wil not be schriven.	So in my pranks I ever will persist;
	Stomak ne conscience know I noon.	Stomach nor conscience truly I have none.
curse	I schrew thes schrifte-fadres, everichoon.	I hate all these shrift-fathers, every one!
	Wel be we met, by God and by seint Jame!	Well met are we, our ways are just the same.
	But, leve brother, telle me thy name?	But, my dear fellow, tell me now your name?"
	Quod this Sompnour. Right § in this menewhile	The Summoner entreated him. Meanwhile
began	This yeman gan a litel for to smyle.	That yeoman broke into a little smile.
wilt thou	Brothir, quod he, woltow that I the telle?	"Brother," he answered, "wilt thou have me tell?

* Tyrwhitt.
† Money forced out of people by threats or ill-usage.
‡ A proverbial expression.
§ Tyrwhitt.

Glossary.	I am a feend, my dwellyng is in helle,	—I am a fiend, my dwelling is in hell,
here	And her I ryde about my purchasyng,	And here I ride about my purchasing
know	To wite wher men wol yive me eny thing.	To know what men will give me anything.
the effect	My purchas is theffect of all my rent.	Such gains make up the whole of all my rent.
	Loke how thou ridest for the same entent	Look how thou journeyest for the same intent
	To wynne good, thou rekkist never how,	To reap thy gains, thou carest never how!
	Right so fare I, for ryde I wolde now	Just so I do—for I will journey now
prey	Unto the worldes ende for a praye.	Unto the wide world's end to get my prey."
ah	A, quod the Sompnour, *benedicite*, what say ye? *	"Mercy!" the Summoner cried, "what is't ye say?"

He is rather aghast at this awful confession, bad as he admits himself to be. He had sincerely thought it was a real yeoman; and when he says to him, with a strange and evil smile, "Shall I tell you?—*I am a fiend, my dwelling is in hell*," the horrible candour strikes him dumb for a minute. He rather wishes he wasn't his sworn brother. But he very soon gets over this, thinking of the gold and silver, and begins to talk quite friendly.

truly	I wende ye were a yemen trewely:	"I thought you were a yeoman, verily:
shape	Ye have a mannes schap as wel as I.	Ye have a human shape as well as I."

"Have you then a distinct form in hell like what I see?"

"No, certainly," says the fiend, "there we have none, but we take a form when we will."

It seem to you	Or ellis make yow seme that we ben schape	"Or else we make you think we have a shape,
	Somtyme like a man, or like an ape;	Sometimes like to a man, or like an ape;
	Or lik an aungel can I ryde or go;	Or like an angel I can ride or go;
	It is no wonder thing though it be so.	It is not wondrous that it should be so."

"Why, a common conjurer can deceive you any day, and I have tenfold more cunning than a conjurer!"

"Why," said the Summoner, quite interested, "do you have several shapes, and not only one?"

"We borrow whatever shape is best to catch our prey," said the evil one.

"What makes you take all that trouble?" says the Summoner.

dear	Ful many a cause, lieve sir Sompnour,	"Full many a cause, my good sir Summoner,"
	Sayde this feend. But al thing hath a tyme;	Replied the fiend. "But all things have a time;
	The day is schort, and it is passed prime, †	The day is short, and it is now past prime,
won	And yit ne wan I nothing in this day;	Yet have I not won anything to-day;
attend	I wol entent to winning, if I may,	I'll give my mind to winning, if I may,
	And not entende our thinges to declare.	And not our privy doings to declare."

For you see the fiend was more intent upon his business than even the Summoner. However, he

---

* Tyrwhitt; more forcible. † The first quarter of the artificial day: i.e. 9 o'clock.

goes on to say, that sometimes he is obliged to work under the great God, without whose sufferance he could never have any power at all.

GLOSSARY.

God's	For somtyme we ben Goddis instrumentes	"Sometimes God uses us as instruments
means	And menes to don his comaundementes,	And means, to work out His all-wise intents:
He chooses	When that Him list, upon His creatures,	When on us this divine command He lays,
various	In divers acts and in divers figures.	We serve in divers forms and divers ways."

"But you needn't be in such a hurry," he says to the Summoner. "You'll know more than you like perhaps before long."

one, jest	But oon thing warne I the, I wol not jape,	"But of one thing I warn thee, not in play,
always know	Thou wilt algates wite how we ben schape.	That thou shalt know what we are like, some day.
	Thou schalt herafterward, my brother deere,	Thou shalt hereafter come, my brother dear,
come, learn	Com wher the nedith not of me to leere, *	Whither thou wilt not need of me to hear;
own	For thou schalt by thin oughn experience	For thou shalt learned be—nay, specially wise
be able, to counsel, meaning	Conne,† in a chayer, reden of this sentence	By self-experience—in these mysteries:
better, alive	Bet than Virgile ‡ when he was on lyve,	Wiser than Virgil ere from earth he past,
quickly	Or Daunt also. Now let us ryde blyve,	Or Dante either. Let us now ride fast,
	For I wol holde companye with the	For I will keep companionship with thee
	Til it be so that thou forsake me.	Till thou desirest to depart from me."

A pleasant prospect! However, the Summoner was quite content, so long as the silver and gold were shared with him. He declares he will never forsake his sworn brother, though he be a fiend, and promises to share all his own goods with the evil one! adding—

thee, give	Tak thou thi part, and that men wil the yyven,	"Take thou thy part, whatever men will give,
mine, live	And I schal myn, thus may we bothe lyven;	And I will do the same, so both shall live;
either	And if that eny of us have more than other,	And if the one get more than doth the other,
	Let him be trewe, and part it with his brother.	Let him be true and share it with his brother."
	I graunte, quod the devel, by my fay.	"I grant it," said the devil, "by my fay."
ride	And with that word thay riden forth hir way.	With that, they rode together on their way.

As they proceeded they saw right at the town's end a cart laden with hay. The road was heavy with mud, so that the cart stuck. The carter smote his horses, and cried like mad, "Hait! go on! § The fiend

---

* Tyrwhitt. Morris has 'nothing for to leere.'

† This verse means, 'You shall hereafter understand this subject so well, as to be able to give lectures on it, as a professor in his chair;' *chayer* being the term for pulpit or professor's chair; *conne* part of the verb conne, to know or be able; and *rede*, to counsel. The evil one is sarcastic on the special wickedness of the Summoner.

‡ Alluding to Eneas' visit to infernal regions (6th book of 'Eneid') and Dante's 'Inferno.'

§ The text has 'Heit, Scot, heit, brok, what spare ye for the stones?' and it is singular that 'hayt' is still the word used by waggoners in Norfolk to make their horses go on; while Scot remains one of the commonest names for a horse in Norfolk and Suffolk. The Reeve's horse in the Prologue is called Scot also. Brock means a badger, hence applied to a grey horse. The carter presently calls this horse 'myn oughne lyard (grey) boy.'

take you—what a labour I have with you. The fiend have it all, cart, horse, and hay!"

The Summoner, hearing this, remembered he was to have half of all the evil one's goods, and whispered to him, "Don't you hear what the carter says? Take it all quick—he has given it you—hay, and cart, and the three horses!"

"Nay," said the evil one, "he does not *mean* what he says. He is only in a passion. Ask him yourself, or else wait and see what comes next."

The carter whacked his horses, and they began to stoop and pull the cart out, and then he said, "Hait! bless you—good Dobbins—well pulled, my own grey boy! Now is my cart out of the mud."

"There, brother, what did I tell you?" says the fiend. "Now, you see the churl said one thing, but he thought another. Let us go on; I shall get nothing here."

With that they went a little way outside the town. The Summoner began to whisper to his companion, "Here there lives an old beldame who would almost as soon lose her head as give up a penny of her goods. But I mean to have twelve pence * out of her, though she should go mad; or else I'll haul her up before the court. And yet, all the same, I know no harm of her. But if you want a lesson how to extort your gains in your country, you may take example of me!"

The Summoner goes and raps at the old widow's gate. "Come out, you old crone. I dare say you are in mischief there!" he cried.

"Who knocks?" said the old woman. "God save you, sir. What is your will?"

"I've a bill of summons against you. On pain of cursing, see that you are to-morrow before the archdeacon, to answer to the court."

"God help me," says the poor old woman, in great distress. "I have been ill a long time, and cannot walk so far, and to ride † would kill me, my side pricks so. May I not ask for a libel, ‡ and answer there by my procurator whatever there is against me?"

"Yes," says the Summoner, "pay me—let's see—twelve pence, and I will let you off. I shall not get much profit out of that. My master gets it, and not I. Make haste and give me twelve pence—I can't wait."

"Twelve pence!" said the poor widow. "Now, heaven help me out of this. I have not so much as twelve pence in the whole wide world. You know that I am old and poor. Rather give me alms."

"Nay, then," cries the hard-hearted Summoner, "I will not let you off, even if you die of it."

"Alas!" says she, "I am not guilty."

"Pay me!" cried he, "or I will carry off your new pan besides, which you owe me, for when you were summoned to the court before, I paid for your punishment!"

"You lie," cried the poor old woman. "I was never summoned before to that court in all my life; and I have done no wrong. May the evil one catch you for your wickedness, and carry you away, and my pan too!"

---

* The value of twelve pence may be estimated by the relative value of food and labour. *Bell* says, "Twelve pence would have bought two dozen hens, or three gallons of red wine, or hired a *dozen* common labourers for *twelve* days," but surely he means a *dozen* labourers for *one* day, or one labourer for twelve days.

† There was then no means of conveyance for people who could not walk except horseback.

‡ A libel, a copy of the information or indictment. A libel is still the expression in the ecclesiastical courts.—*Bell*. The abuses, we see, have led to another interpretation of the word libel—as *libellous*.

And when the fiend heard her curse the Summoner on her knees, he came forward and said, "Now, good mother, are you in earnest when you say that?"

"May the devil fetch him, pan and all, before he dies, if he doesn't repent!"

"Repent!" cries the wicked Summoner, "I don't mean to repent anything I do, I can tell you. I wish I had everything you possess besides—even every rag you have on!"

"Now, brother," says the evil one, "don't be angry; for you and this pan are mine by right. This very night you shall go with me to hell, and you will soon know more about our mysteries than a master of divinity!"

GLOSSARY.

caught	And with that word the foule fend him hente;	With that the foul fiend took him for his own,
	Body and soule, he with the devyl wente,	Body and soul he's with the devil gone,
their	Wher as the Sompnours han her heritage;	Whither these Summoners have their heritage
made	And God, that maked after His ymage	And God, who did create in His image
	Mankynde, save and gyde us alle and some,	Mankind, protect and guide us all our days,
grant	And leene this Sompnour good man to bycome.	And lead this Summoner here to mend his ways.

Lordings, I could have told you, if I had time, all the pains and punishments which came to this wicked Summoner in hell. But let us all pray to be kept from the tempter's power. The lion lies in wait always to slay the innocent, if he can. Dispose your hearts ever to withstand the evil fiend who longs to make you his slaves! He will not tempt you above what you can bear, for Christ will be your champion and your knight. * And pray that this Summoner with us, may repent of his misdeeds before the devil carries him away.

Notes by the Way.

LEGENDS of the kind told by the Friar were very popular in the mediæval times, believed in by some as they were laughed at by others. Mr. Wright conjectures that this tale was translated from some old fabliau. The Friar evidently counted on the unpopularity of this class of men, the Summoners, when he held his fellow-traveller up to general ignominy in this way. It seems a breach of civility and fair-play to modern minds, but the Summoners were in reality hated universally for their extortion or for their secret power among the people. As you have seen, the host begins by calling for justice, but the popular feeling was but too clearly on the Friar's side from the first, and mine host shares it. (*Vide* notes, pp. 31, 57.)

This Tale would appear by no means to discourage swearing; but mark the distinction drawn between a hearty, deliberate malediction, and the rapid unmeaning oath which sowed the common talk. The lesson was probably the more forcible through the absence of any hypercritical censure of 'strong language'—censure which would have been vain indeed, in an age when common oaths were thought as much less of, as positive cursing was more of, than in the present day.

The rough moral deduced was admirably suited to the coarse and ignorant minds of the lower orders.

---

* This singular (to us) term as applied to Christ, was of course borrowed from the popular notion of warfare, when each knight, inspired by some fair inciter, was the more valiant for her sake. The term is both picturesque and forcible as an appeal to the common understanding, in which the Friars were naturally adepts.

THE CLERK'S TALE.

Glossary.		
	THIS Sompnour in his styrop up he stood,	Up in his stirrups did the Summoner start,
mad	Upon the Frere his herte was so wood	For with this Friar such rage was in his heart,
quaked	That lyk an aspen leef he quok for ire.	That like an aspen-leaf he shook for ire.
	Lordyngs, quod he, but oon thing I desire;	"Lordings," cried he, "but one thing I desire,
	I yow biseke that of your curtesye,	And I beseech you of your courtesy,
	Syn ye han herd this false Frere lye,	Since you have heard this falsest Friar lie,
pray suffer	As suffrith me, I may my tale telle.	Suffer me, pray, my story now to tell.
	This Frere bosteth that he knowith helle,	This Friar boasts of how he knoweth hell;
	And God it wot, that is but litel wonder, *	Heav'n knows, that if he does it is no wonder,
	Freres and feendes been but litel asonder. †	For fiends and Friars are not far asunder."

Oxford	Sir Clerk of Oxenford, our hoste sayde,	"Sir Clerk of Oxford," then our landlord said
	Ye ryde as stille and coy as doth a mayde ‡	"You ride as shy and quiet as a maid
	Were newe spoused, syttyng at the bord; §	Newly espous'd, who sits beside the board;
	This day ne herde I of your mouth a word.	All day we have not had from you a word.
sophism	I trow ye study aboute som sophyme.	I guess, some subtle lore you're studying.
	But Salomon saith, everythyng hath tyme.	But Solomon says there's time for everything.
be	For Goddis sake as beth of better cheere,	Prithee, rouse up, and be of better cheer,
study	It is no tyme for to stodye hiere.	It is no time for your deep studies here.

"Do not give us a sermon, or something so learned that we cannot understand it.

Spekith so playn at this tyme, we yow praye,	"Speak to us very plainly, now, we pray,
That we may understonde that ye saye.	That we may understand the whole you say."

* Tyrwhitt.
† The Summoner's Tale (omitted) follows here.
‡ Students then entered the university at a far younger age than at the present day, almost indeed when boys now enter the public schools, so that the Clerk of Oxford may have been but a boy, which would account for his diffident demeanour: yet his education and knowledge might warrant mine host's fear of his being too learned for them.
§ Table: a board upon trestles.

This worthy Clerk answered pleasantly, "Host, I am under your orders, so I will obey you, and tell you a tale which I learned at Padua, of a worthy clerk, who has been proved by his words and work.

GLOSSARY.

coffin	He is now deed and nayled in his chest,	"Now he is dead, and nailéd in his chest,
give	Now God yive his soule wel good rest!	I pray to God to give his spirit rest!
	Fraunces Petrark * the laureat poete,	Francis Petrarch, the poet laureate,
was named	Highte this clerk, whos rethorique swete	This clerk was call'd, whose rhetoric sweet did late
Italy	Enlumynd al Ytail of poetrie,	Illume all Italy with poetry,
	As Linian † did of philosophie,	As Linian did with his philosophy,
law	Or lawue, or other art particulere;	And law, and other noble arts as well;
	But deth, that wol not suffre us duellen here,	But death, that will not suffer us here to dwell,
eye	But as it were a twyncling of an ye,	But, as it were, a twinkling of an eye,
	Hem bothe hath slayn, and alle schul we dye.	Hath slain them both, and we, too, all shall die."

PART I.

TO the west of Italy there is a territory called Saluces,‡ which once belonged to a marquis very much beloved by all his people. They all obeyed and respected him, both lords and commoners, and he was very happy.

Besides, he was the noblest born of any one in Lombardy—handsome, and strong, and young—courteous to all, and discreet enough, except in some things where he was not quite perfect! and his name was Walter.

The worst fault of him was the careless sort of life he led. He did nothing but hunt, and hawk, and amuse himself, instead of attending to more serious duties. This made his people very sorry, and they thought if Walter had a wife he would get more steady, and not waste his time so sadly.

One day all his people went in a great crowd to see him; and the wisest one among them said—"O noble marquis, your goodness gives us courage to come to you and tell you what we want. Do not be angry, but deign to listen to us, for we all love you. The only thing needed to make us quite happy is for you to marry. We pray you, then, to let us find you a nice wife, and we will choose the noblest and best in the land."

Walter listened, and then answered—"My dear people, you know I am very comfortable as I am, and enjoy my liberty: I don't want a wife. But if it makes you any happier, I will try and get one as soon as I can. As for choosing me one, pray don't take so much trouble. I would much rather do that for myself. Only remember that when I am married, you must always show the greatest honour and respect to whoever she may be. For since I consent to give up my freedom to please you, you must not find fault with any one whom I choose."

---

* These are the lines on which the supposition is based that Petrarch and Chaucer had met.

† "Joannes of Lignano, near Milan, a canonist and natural philosopher, who flourished about 1378."—B.

‡ Saluzzo, a marquisate near Mount Viso: Lat. Vesulus.

THE CLERK'S TALE

All the people promised they would be quite content with any wife he liked, for they were so much afraid he would not marry at all if they didn't.

Then, to make quite sure, they begged him to fix exactly the day when the wedding should take place, and he did so, promising to get everything ready, according to their request. And the people thanked him on their knees and went away.

Part II.

NOW, near the marquis's palace, there was a village in which dwelt a poor man—poorer than the poorest of his neighbours. His name was Janicula, and he had a young daughter who was fair enough to see, called Griselda.

But, in beauty of mind, Griselda was the fairest maiden under the sun. She had been brought up very humbly, and more often drank water than wine, and she worked so hard that she was never idle.

GLOSSARY.

	But though this mayden tender were of age,	But though this maiden was as yet so young,
breast, girlhood	Yet in the brest of her virginité	Under her girlish innocence there lay
mature, serious	Ther was enclosed rype and sad corrage; *	A brave and serious spirit, ever strong;
love	And in gret reverence and charité	And with good heart she laboured day by day
	Hir olde pore fader fostered sche;	To tend and help her father, poor and grey.
field	A fewe scheep spynnyng on the feld sche kepte,	Some sheep while spinning in the fields she kept,
would not be	Sche nolde not ben ydel til sche slepte.	For never was she idle till she slept.
came bring	And when sche hom-ward com, sche wolde brynge	And she would often, as she homeward sped,
worts	Wortis or other herbis tymes ofte,	Bring with her herbs and cresses gathered there,
chop, boil living	The which sche schred and seth for her lyvynge,	Which for a meal she fain would seethe and shred.
	And made hir bed ful hard, and nothing softe.	Hard was her bed and frugal was her fare,
ever, supported	And ay sche kept hir fadres lif on lofte	Keeping her father with untiring care,
	With every obeissance and diligence,	And all obedience, and all diligence
father's	That child may do to fadres reverence.	That child can give to filial reverence.

On this poor hard-working Griselda, the marquis Walter had often cast his eyes when he happened to pass her while hunting. And when he looked at her it was with no foolish thoughts, but with serious admiration for her virtue. He had never seen any one so young who was so good, and he made up his mind if ever he married anybody he would marry her.

So, after the people's visit, according to his promise to them, Walter began to prepare beautiful dresses

---

* *Corage* is used in several senses: impulse (as in the opening lines of the Prologue), feeling, or disposition may be implied. The word is derived from the Latin *cor*, the heart.

and jewels, brooches and rings of gold, and everything proper for a great lady. And the wedding-day arrived, but no one had seen any bride, or could think where she was to come from!

At last all the feast was ready, all the palace beautifully adorned, upstairs and downstairs—hall and chambers. The noble guests arrived who were bidden to the wedding—lords and ladies richly arrayed—and still there was no bride!

The marquis made them all follow him into the village, to the sound of music.

Now, Griselda, who knew nothing of all this, went that morning to fetch water from the well; and she heard say that this was to be the marquis's wedding-day.

So she hastened home, and thought to herself she would get through her work as fast as she could, and try to see something of the sight.

"I will stand with the other girls at the door," she said to herself innocently, "and I shall see the new marchioness, if she passes by this way to the castle."

Just as she crossed the door, the marquis came up, and called her.

Griselda set down her water-cans beside the door in an ox's stall, * and, dropping on her knees, † waited for the great lord to speak.

The marquis said gravely, "Where is thy father, Griselda?" and Griselda answered humbly, "He is all ready here," and hurried in to fetch him.

Then the marquis took the poor man by the hand, saying, "Janicula, I shall no longer hide the wish of my heart. If you will consent, I will take your daughter for my wife before I leave this house. I know you love me, and are my faithful liegeman. Tell me, then, whether you will have me for your son-in-law."

This sudden offer so astonished the poor man that he grew all red, and abashed, and trembling. He could say nothing but—"My lord, it is not for me to gainsay your lordship. Whatever my lord wishes."

GLOSSARY.

yet	Yit wol I, quod this markys softly,	"Yet," said the marquis, softly, "fain would I
meeting, knowest thou	That in thy chambre, I and thou and sche Have a collacioun, and wostow why?	That in thy chamber I and thou and she Confer together—dost thou wonder why?
	For I wol aske if that it hir wille be	For I would ask her whether she will be
according to	To be my wyf, and reule hir after me;	My wife—and rule herself to pleasure me;
done	And al this schal be doon in thy presence,	And in thy presence all things shall be said:
hearing	I wol nought speke out of thyn audience.	Behind thy back no contract shall be made."

And while the three were talking in the chamber all the people came into the house without, ‡ and wondered among themselves how carefully and kindly she kept her father. But poor Griselda, who had never seen such a sight before, looked quite pale. She was not used to such grand visitors.

---

* See note ‡ below.

† The courtsey of modern times is all that remains of the old custom of kneeling.

‡ The house without. In these early times, dwelling-places were usually built within a court. The court was, among the poor, a spot enclosed by a hedge or fence of sticks, and often a dry ditch; in the middle of this enclosure or house, the *hall* in which they lived stood—a mere covered room. The chamber or *bower*, for sleeping and privacy, was a second erection within the court; but, in the case of so poor a man as Janicula, probably there was but one covered room, hall *or* chamber, used for any purpose of shelter. So when the guests came into the *house* without, the enclosure is meant, within which a single hut stood, built of planks. Janicula's ox (used for draught, as now in Italy) inhabited the hut with them, and Griselda sets down her can in the stall when she enters the hut. In and around Naples we may still see the turkeys, pigs, and donkeys sharing the hovels with the peasants in this miserable way.

GRISELDA'S MARRIAGE

'This is ynough, Grisilde myn, quod he.'

This is what the marquis said to her.

"Griselda, it pleases your father and me that I should marry you, and I suppose you will not be unwilling.* But first I must ask you, since it is to be done in such a hurry, will you say yes now, or will you think it over? Are you ready to obey me in all things when you are my wife, whether I am kind to you or not? and never to say no when I say yes—either by word or by frowns? Swear that, and I will swear to marry you."

Wondering at all this, and trembling with fear, Griselda answered—

"My lord, I am quite unworthy of the great honour you offer me; but whatever my lord wishes I will consent to. And I will swear never, so far as I know, to disobey you—not even if you wish to kill me, though I don't want to die."

"That is enough, my Griselda," said Walter, and he went gravely out at the door, and showed her to the people. "This is my wife, who stands here," he said: "honour and love her, whoever loves me."

Then, so that she might not enter his castle in her poor gown, he bade all the gentlewomen robe her at once in beautiful clothes; and though these smart ladies did not much like touching the old clothes she had on, still they stript them all off her, and clad her all new and splendidly, from head to foot.

Then they combed and dressed her hair, which was quite loose and disarranged, and with their delicate fingers they placed a crown on her head, and covered her with jewels, great and small. They hardly knew her, so beautiful she looked when she was thus richly attired.

The marquis put a ring on her finger, which he had brought on purpose, and set her on a snow-white horse; and she was conducted, with great rejoicings, to the palace, where the day was spent in feasting and merriment till the sun set. †

In short, heaven so favoured the new marchioness, that in a little time you would never have guessed she was of so humble birth; she might have been brought up in an emperor's hall, and not in a hut with oxen. The people who had known her from her childhood could hardly believe she was Janicle's daughter, she was so changed for the better.

Moreover, her virtue and gentle dignity made her beloved by everybody, so that her fame was spread throughout all the country, and people even took long journeys to come and look upon her.

Walter had not a fault to find with her. She made him happy by her excellence and her wifely homeliness, just as she made the people happy by her kindness and cleverness in redressing their wrongs.

Part III.

GRISELDA had a little girl at last, which was a great joy to them both, and to all the people. But Walter had a great longing to put his wife to the test—to see whether she was really as meek and patient and submissive as she seemed.

I know not why he wanted to do this, for he had often tried her in little ways before, and had found

---

* On the Continent, even at the present day, the bride is *expected* to assent to the bridegroom chosen by her parents. Walter treated Griselda with especial consideration and respect by consulting her. Skeat quotes the legal formula of refusal, *Le roy s'avisera*, to show that Walter's question, "Wol ye assent, or elles yoe avyse?" gave her the chance to refuse.

† In the 14th century it was the custom for everybody to go to bed with the sun. They rose in the morning at 4 or 5, had breakfast at 6, dinner at 10 or 11, and supper about 6.

her perfect; and for my part I think it is a cruel deed to grieve and torment a wife who does not deserve it, for the sake of needless proof.

However, Walter did as follows. One night, while the baby was still very young, he came to her, looking stern and troubled; she was all alone, and he said, "Griselda, you have not forgotten the day when I took you out of your poor home. Well, although you are very dear to me, to my people you are not dear; they feel it a great shame to be the subjects of one who came of such mean rank. And since thy daughter was born they have murmured so greatly that I cannot disregard them, so I must do with the baby as the people choose, if I want to live in peace with them all. Yet what I must do is much against my will, and I will not do it without your consent; but I pray you to show me now how patient you can be, even as you swore to be, on our marriage day."

When Griselda heard this she did not know that it was all untrue, and she said calmly, "My lord, all shall be as you will. My child and I, we are both yours, living or dying. Do as you choose. For my part, there is nothing I fear to lose, but *you*."

The marquis was overjoyed to hear that, but he concealed his pleasure, and kept a very stern and sad face, and presently departed.

He went to a man, to whom he gave certain directions how to act; then he sent the man to Griselda.

This man was a sergeant, * the trusted servant of the marquis, and he stalked into Griselda's chamber. "Madam," he said, "you must forgive me if I do what I am compelled to by my lord. This child I am ordered to take away," and the man made as though he would kill it at once.

GLOSSARY.

ill-fame	Suspecious was the defame of this man,	Suspicious of repute was this stern man,
	Suspect his face, suspect his word also,	Suspicious in his look, and speech also,
	Suspect the tyme in which he this bigan.	So was the time when he the deed began.
	Allas! hir doughter, that she lovede so,	Alas! her baby, that she lovëd so,
believed, then	Sche wende he wold han slayen it right tho;	Would he destroy it ere he turned to go?—
nevertheless, sighed	But natheles sche neyther weep ne sikede,	And yet she did not weep, she was resign'd
	Conformyng hir to that the marquis likede.	To all the wishes of her master's mind.
to speak	But atte laste speke sche bigan,	To say a few meek words she then began,
	And mekely sche to the sergeant preyde,	And for one boon she pitifully pray'd,
	So as he was a worthy gentil man,	That as he was a kind and worthy man
might	That she moste kisse hir child er that it deyde.	She might but kiss her baby ere it died.
lap	And in hir barm * this litel child sche leyde,	And in her lap the little child she laid,
	With ful sad face, and gan the child to blesse,	With mournful face, and did the baby bless,
began, kiss	And lullyd it, and after gan it kesse.	And lull'd it with how many a soft caress!

And then she said, in her gentle voice, "Farewell, my child; I shall never see thee again; but since I have marked thee with the cross, may He who died for us all bless thee! To him, little child, I give thy soul, for this night thou shalt die for my sake."

* Sergeant and servant are doublets.—*Skeat*. Probably he was a cross between a highwayman and a soldier.

Sergeant at one time meant squire to a prince or nobleman. †Tyrwhitt.

Truly, even to a nurse, this would have been hard to bear, but to a mother how far more grievous! Still she was so firm and brave that she soon gave up the baby to the sergeant, saying, "Take the little, tiny maid, and go, do my lord's command. But one thing I pray you, that when it is dead you will bury the little body in some place where birds and beasts will not mangle it."

The sergeant would not promise her even that, but carried the child off with him. *

He took the babe to the marquis, and told him exactly all that Griselda had said. The marquis certainly showed some little feeling and regret; yet he kept to his purpose, as men will when they are determined. He then bade the sergeant wrap up the child softly and tenderly, and carry it in secret, in a box or the skirt of a garment, to Bologna, where dwelt his sister, Countess of Panik. † She would foster it kindly; but whom the child belonged to was to be kept from all men's knowledge.

The sergeant did as he was commanded, and the marquis watched his wife to see if there should be any rebellion in her manner. But she did not change. She was always kind, and loving, and serious, and as busy and humble as ever. Not a word she spoke of the poor baby.

Part IV.

A FEW years afterwards, Griselda had another child—a little boy. This was still more joy to the people and to Walter than the other baby, because it was the heir.

When the babe was two years old, the marquis took it into his head to tempt again his poor wife. Ah! how needless to torture her! but married men care for no limits when they find a patient wife!

"Wife," said the marquis, "I have told you how discontented are the people with our marriage; and since the boy's birth their anger has been greater. Their murmuring destroys all my comfort and courage. They grumble, because when I am dead the blood of Janicle shall succeed to my heritage; and I cannot disregard the words they say! So I think I will serve him as I served his sister; but do not suddenly fly out with grief. Be patient, I beg of you, and command your feelings."

Griselda answered, sadly and calmly, when she heard this—

Glossary.		
	I have, quod sche, sayd thus, and ever schal,	"I have," quoth she, "said this, and ever shall,
will not	I wol no thing, ne nil no thing certayn,	I wish not, nor will wish, it is certain,
please	But as yow list: nought greveth me at al,	But as you choose: I grieve me not at all,
	Though that my doughter and my sone be slayn	Although my daughter and my son be slain
say	At your comaundement: this is to sayn,	At your commandment: nor will I complain
	I have not had no part of children twayne,	That I have had no part in children twain,
sickness	But first syknes, and after wo and payne.	But sickness first, and then a bitterer pain.
be, master	Ye ben oure lord: doth with your owne thing	"Thou art our lord: do, then, with what is thine
ask, advice	Right as yow list: axith no red of me;	E'en as thou wilt: ask not assent of me;—
	For as I left at hom al my clothing	For as I left at home all that was mine

---

* It was common, nay usual, in mediæval times for noble children to be put out to nurse in the family of some equal or dependent, for purposes of security. The removal of Walter's children from the mother was *not* an outrage: but concealing their fate from her was.

† *Panico*, Petrarch; *Panigo*, Boccace. I cannot be sure of the situation of this place, but there is a certain Paganico near Urbino, marked in old maps as a castle or fortress, which is not too far from Bologna to be possibly the place referred to. A river Panaro flows between Modena and Bologna.

Glossary		
	Whan I first com to yow, right so, quod sche,	When I came first to thee, right so," quoth she,
	Left I my wille and al my liberte,	"Left I my will and all my liberty,
you	And took your clothing; wherfor, I yow preye	And took new habits: wherefore, now, I pray
desire	Doth your plesaunce, I wil youre lust obeye.	Do but thy pleasure, and I will obey."

"If I knew beforehand what your wish was," said poor Griselda, "I would do it without delay; but now that I know your will, I am ready to die if you desire it; for death is nothing compared with your love!"

When the marquis heard that, he cast down his eyes, and wondered how she could endure it all; and he went forth looking very dreary, but in reality he felt extremely pleased.

The ugly sergeant came again, and took away the little boy: Griselda kissed it and blessed it, only asking that his little limbs might be kept from the wild beasts and birds; but the sergeant promised nothing, and secretly took him with great care to Bologna.

The marquis was amazed at her patience; for he knew that, next to himself, she loved her children best of anything in the world. What could he do more to prove her steadfastness, and faithfulness, and patience? But there are some people who, when they have once taken a thing into their head, will stick to it as if they were bound to a stake. So this marquis made up his mind to try his wife still further.

He watched her closely, but never could he find any change in her: the older she grew, the more faithful and industrious she was. Whatever he liked, she liked: there seemed but one will between them; and, God be thanked, all was for the best.

But all this time the slander against Walter spread far and near; and the people said he had wickedly murdered both his children, because his wife was a poor woman. For the people had no idea what had really become of them. And they began to hate Walter instead of loving him, as they had once done; for a murderer is a hateful name.

Still the marquis was so determined to test his wife, that he cared for nothing else.

When Griselda's daughter was twelve years old, Walter sent secretly to Rome, commanding that false letters, seeming to come from the Pope, should be made according to his will. These letters, or 'bulls,' were to give him leave to quit his first wife, for the sake of his people, and marry another woman; but they were none of them really from the Pope: they were all counterfeit and false, made by Walter's order, to deceive Griselda.

The common people did not know the difference between true letters and false; but when the tidings arrived, Griselda was very sorrowful; for she loved Walter best of all things, as he very well knew.

judge, sad	I deeme that hir herte was ful wo; *	Full sure am I her heart was full of wo;
alike, firm	But sche, ylike sad for evermo,	But she, as though serene for evermo,
disposed	Disposid was, this humble creature,	Was ready, in her humbleness of mind,
fortune, to endure	Th'adversite of fortun al tendure.	In all adversity to be resign'd.

* Tyrwhitt.

GRISELDA'S SORROW

'And as a lamb sche sitteth meeke and stille,
And let this cruel sergeant doon his wille.'

THE CLERK'S TALE

Then the marquis sent to the Earl of Panik, who had married his sister, begging him to bring both his children home, openly and in great honour; but no one was to know whose children they were. He was to answer no questions—

G<small>LOSSARY</small>.

Glossary	Middle English	Modern
should	But saye the mayde schuld i-wedded be *	But say the maiden should, ere long, be wed
immediately	Unto the Markys of Saluce anoon.	Unto the Marquis of Saluce so high.
did	And as this eorl was prayd, so dede he;	And as this earl was pray'd to do, he did,
gone	For at day set he on his way is goon	And started on his journey speedily
many a one	Toward Saluce, and lordes many oon,	Towards Saluces, with lordly company
	In riche array, this mayden for to guyde,	In rich array, this maiden fair to guide,
	Hir yonge brother rydyng by hir syde.	Her little brother riding by her side.
	Arrayed was toward hir mariage	And this fresh maid was robed for marriage
maiden, gems	This freisshe may, al ful of gemmes clere;	Full of clear gems, in goodly raiment rare;
	Hir brother, which that seven yer was of age,	Her brother, who was seven years of age,
also, manner	Arrayed eek ful freissh in his manere;	Was in his fashion clad all fresh and fair;
nobleness	And thus in gret noblesse and with glad chere,	And thus, in splendour, and with joyous air,
their	Toward Saluces shaping her journay,	Towards Saluces following the way,
their	Fro day to day thay ryden in her way.	The cavalcade advances day by day.

P<small>ART</small> V.

I<small>N</small> order to put the last trial upon Griselda, to the uttermost proof of her courage, the marquis one day, before all the household, said to her in a boisterous way—

Glossary	Middle English	Modern
certainly, pleasure	Certes, Grisildes, I had y-nough plesaunce	"Tis true, Griselda, I was once content
	To have yow to my wif, for your goodnesse	To marry you—because you were so good,
truth, obedience	And for youre trouthe, and for your obeissaunce;	And true, and faithful, and obedient—
lineage, wealth	Nought for your lignage, ne for your richesse;	Not for your wealth, nor for your noble blood;
truth	But now know I in verray sothfastnesse	Still one thing must be clearly understood,
am not mistaken	That in gret lordschip, if I wel avyse,	That in this rank and riches men so praise
sundry wise	Ther is gret servitude in sondry wyse.	There is great servitude in many ways.
	I may not do, as every ploughman may;	"I may not do as every ploughman may:
constrain	My poeple me constreignith for to take	My people urge me evermore to take
	Another wyf, and crien day by day;	Another wife, and clamour day by day.
	And eek the Pope, rancour for to slake,	And now the Pope, their rancour swift to slake,
dare	Consentith it, that dar I undertake;	Gives glad consent to any change I make;

* It was not uncommon in olden times for girls to be married at twelve years of age.

Glossary		
much	And trewely, thus moche I wol yow saye,	And more than that—I need not fear to say—
	My newe wif is comyng by the waye.	My new wife is already on her way.
heart	Be strong of hert, and voyde anoon hir place,	Make way for her, be brave, give up her place,
that	And thilke dower that ye broughten me	And, see, the dowry that you brought to me
	Tak it agayn, I graunt it of my grace.	I will restore—I grant it of my grace.
return	Retourneth to your fadres hous, quod he,	Go back unto your father's house," quoth he,
	No man may alway have prosperité,	"No one can always have prosperity.
advise	With even hert I rede yow endure	With equal spirit suffer weal or woe,
chance	The strok of fortune or of adventure.	The gifts of chance or luck that come and go."
	And sche agayn answerd in paciènce:	And she replied, with perfect patience:
	My lord, quod sche, I wot, and wist alway,	"My lord, I know, and knew alway," quoth she,
	How that bitwixe your magnificence	"Too well, that 'tween your own magnificence
nobody	And my poverté, no wight can ne may	And my great poverty, there cannot be
	Make comparisoun, it is no nay;	Comparison at all, and verily
worthy, manner	I ne held me neuer digne in no manere	I held myself unworthy every way
chambermaid	To ben your wif, ne yit your chamberere.	To be your wife—or servant—for a day.
	And in this hous, ther ye me lady made,	"And in this house wherein ye made me great
	(The highe God take I for my witnesse,	(High God my witness, who shall haply set
cheer	And al-so wisly he my soule glade)	Some coming comfort in my altered state),
	I never huld me lady ne maistresse,	Lady nor mistress never was I yet;
	But humble servaunt to your worthinesse,	But humble servant to the grace I get:
life	And ever schal, whil that my lyf may dure,	This I shall be, with spirit ever strong,
above	Aboven every worldly creature.	More than all others, yea, my whole life long.
benignity	That ye so longe of your benignité	"And for your charity in keeping me
nobleness	Han holden me in honour and nobleye,	In dignity and honour day by day
where	Wher as I was not worthy for to be,	So many years, unworthy though I be,
thank	That thonk I God and yow, to whom I preye	Now thank I God and you, to whom I pray
repay	For-yeld it yow, ther is no more to seye.	That He will all your graciousness repay.
go	Unto my fader gladly wil I wende,	Unto my father cheerfully I wend
	And with him duelle unto my lyves ende.	To dwell with him from now to my life's end.
	Ther I was fostred as a child ful smal,	"There I was fostered as an infant small,
	Til I be deed my lyf ther wil I lede,	There till I die my life I will lead through,
clean	A widow clene in body, hert, and al:	Dwell as an honest widow, heart and all.
since, maidenhood	For sith I yaf to yow my maydenhede,	For since I gave my girlhood unto you,
	And am your trewe wyf, it is no drede,	And am your wife, most loving and most true,

THE CLERK'S TALE

Glossary.		
shield (forbid)	God schilde such a lordes wyf to take	It were not fitting that a great lord's wife
for, for mate	Another man to housbond or to make.	Should wed another husband all her life.

	And of your newe wif, God of his grace	"And with your wife to be, God of his grace
	So graunte yow wele and prosperité,	Grant you all welfare and prosperity;
yield	For I wol gladly yelden hir my place,	For I will yield her cheerfully my place,
	In which that I was blisful wont to be.	In which I once so happy used to be;
	For sith it liketh yow, my lord, quod sche,	For since it pleaseth you, my lord," quoth she,
once	That whilom were al myn hertes reste,	"Who ever were the dearest to my heart,
please	That I schal gon, I wol go whan yow leste.	That I should go, content I will depart.

proffer	But ther as ye profre me such dowayre	"But when you bid me take again that dower
	As I ferst brought, it is wel in my mynde,	That I first brought, it still is in my mind:
wretched	It were my wrecchid clothes, no thing faire,	It was my wretched clothing, coarse and poor—
	The whiche to me were hard now for to fynde.	Rags that it were not easy now to find.
	O goode God! how gentil and how kynde	And, O good God! how gentle and how kind
speech	Ye semede by your speche and your visage,	You then seemed, by your words and by your look,
made	That day that maked was our mariage!	That day whereon the name of wife I took!"

Griselda said no word of reproach to her cruel husband, except one touching remark, which he may have felt as one—

"Love is not old as when that it is new." (Love is not the same in after years as when it first comes.)

Then she appeals to him in a way that must have touched a heart of stone, for she saw no sign of relenting in his face: she does not know how far his brutality will go, and will not be surprised at the last insult.

	My lord, ye wot that in my fadres place	"My lord, you know that in my father's place
strip, attire	Ye dede me strippe out of my pore wede,	You stript me of my poor attire, for ruth:
	And richely me cladden of your grace;	Anew you richly clad me, of your grace.
else	To yow brought I nought elles, out of drede,	And I brought nothing unto you, in truth,
maidenhood	But faith, and nakednesse, and maydenhede;	But honesty, and poverty, and youth.
	And her agayn my clothyng I restore,	And here again your clothing I restore,
	And eek my weddyng ryng for evermore.	And ev'n your wedding-ring for evermore.

remainder	The remenant of your jewels redy be	"The remnant of your jewels ready be
dare	Within your chambur, dar I saufly sayn.	Within your chamber, I can safely say.
	Naked out of my fadres hous, quod sche,	With nothing from my father's house," quoth she,

return	I com, and naked moot I torne agayn.	"I came, with nothing I shall go away.
follow gladly	Al your pleisauns wold I folwen fayn; *	In all things as you bid I will obey;
intention	But yit I hope it be not youre entente,	But yet I hope you will not let me go
smockless, palace	That I smocles out of your paleys wente.	Quite as bereft as when I came to you."

A faint sparkle of human spirit comes into her entreaty—"Ye could not do so dishonest (shameful) a thing:"—

own	Remembre yow, myn oughne lord so deere,	"Remember yet, my lord and husband dear,
	I was your wyf, though I unworthy were.	I was your wife, though I unworthy were!
girlhood	Wherfor, in guerdoun of my maydenhede,	"Thus, in requital of the youth I brought,
carry away	Which that I brought, and not agayn I bere,	But never can take back, nor have it more,
vouchsafe, reward	As vouchethsauf as yeve me to my meede	Give me, I pray, a garment of such sort
smock, wear	But such a smok as I was wont to were.	As in those days of poverty I wore."

Walter accepts this humble claim; mark the calm dignity with which she refrains from giving way before her 'folk.'

smock	The smok,† quod he, that thou hast on thy bak,	"The shift," he said, "thou hast upon thy back,
	Let it be stille, and ber it forth with the.	Let it remain, and bear it forth with thee."
scarcely, this	But wel unnethes thilke word he spak,	But scarcely that hard word for pain he spake,
compassion	But went his way for routhe and for pité.	And went his way for sorrow and pity.
herself	Byforn the folk hirselven strippith sche,	Before the household all her robes stript she;
head and feet	And in hir smok, with heed and foot al bare,	And in her shift, barefoot and bare of head,
went	Toward hir fader house forth is she fare.	Toward her father's house forth is she sped.
follow her	The folk hir folwen wepyng in hir weye,	The household follow, tears in every eye,
curse	And fortune ay thay cursen as thay goon;	Bewailing her ill-fortune as they go;
dry	But she fro wepyng kept hir eyen dreye,	But she from weeping kept her own eyes dry,
none	Ne in this tyme word ne spak sche noon.	Nor spake a word to those who murmur'd so.
	Hir fader, that this tyding herd anoon,	Her father heard the news awhile ago,
	Cursede the day and tyme that nature	And sore laments the day that he was born,
formed, living	Schoop him to ben a lyves creäture.	To be a thing so helpless and forlorn.
	For oute of doute this olde pore man	For ever without doubt the poor old man
suspicion	Was ever in suspect of hir mariage;	Distrusted heartily her altered rank;
believed	For ever he deemede, sith that it bigan,	Believing inly since it first began,
	That whan the lord fulfilled had his corrage,	That when my lord had wearied of his prank,

* Skeat.　　　　† The smock, or shift, was a high garment with long sleeves, often embroidered with black stitchery.

Glossary		
disparagement	Him wolde thinke that it were disparage	He would conceive it far beneath his rank
	To his estate, so lowe for to lighte,	To have a low-born wife, however good,
put her away	And voyden hire as sone as ever he mighte.	And rid himself of her whene'er he could.
goeth	Agayns his doughter hastily goth he	Unto his daughter hastily he goes,
	(For he by noyse of folk knew hir comyng),	(For by the noise of crowds he knew her nigh),
coat	And with hir olde cote, as it might be,	And her old garb about her form he throws,
sorrowfully	He covered hir, ful sorwfully wepynge,	And covers her, with tears and many a sigh,
	But on hir body might he it nought bringe,	But could not draw it round her properly,
coarse, more	For rude was the cloth, and mor of age,	For coarse and shrunk the cloth was—worse for age
many (viel)	By dayes fele than at hir mariage.	By many days, than at her marriage.
	Thus with hir fader for a certeyn space	Thus with her father for a certain space
flower	Dwellith this flour of wifly pacience,	Did dwell this flower of wifely patience;
	That neyther by hir wordes, ne by hir face,	And neither by her speech nor by her face,
also, their	Byforn the folk nor eek in her absence,	Before the folk, nor e'en in their absènce,
showed, done	Ne schewed sche that hir was doon offence;	Seem'd she to feel that she endured offence.
nor, estate	Ne of hir highe astaat no remembraunce	As far as any living soul could see
	Ne hadde she, as by hir countenaunce.	She had of her past state no memory.

And after all it was scarce any wonder. For in her days of wealth her spirit had always been humble and meek. No dainty fare, no foolish pomp or luxury, no semblance of splendid rank, had she allowed herself; but, ever wise and humble and firm, when reverses came she was ready to bear them.

Men speak of Job's patience; but, though some praise women little enough, no man can be as patient as a woman can—no man be faithful as a woman can.

Part VI.

At last the Earl of Panik arrived, whose fame had been spreading among great and small. The people had all found out that he was bringing them a new marchioness, in such pomp and state, that never before had a like splendour been seen throughout West Lombardy.

The marquis, who had arranged all these things, sent for this poor innocent Griselda; and she came with humble mind and joyful face, and no proud notions in her heart, and knelt before him and asked his will.

"Griselda," he said, "my will is that the maiden whom I am to marry be received here as royally as it is possible in my house to be, and that everybody, according to his degree, shall be made thoroughly welcome and happy. I have no woman able to arrange my rooms fully to my liking, and therefore I want you to take everything in hand. You know of old my ways and my tastes; therefore, though your dress is ragged and you look very bad, you must do your duties to the very best of your power."

Griselda answered, "Not only, lord, am I glad to do anything for you, but I love you enough to work all my days to please you."

And with that worde sche gan the hous to dighte,	And with that word she 'gan the house to deck,
And tables for to sette, and beddes make:	To set the tables and to make the beds:

begging all the chambermaids to hasten and hurry and shake and sweep smartly; and she, most serviceable of them all, got every chamber and the great hall garnished and adorned.

GLOSSARY.

forenoon	Abouten undern gan this lord alighte,	Somewhat ere noonday did this earl alight,
two	That with him broughte these noble children tweye;	Who with him brought the unknown children fair,
	For which the peple ran to se that sighte	And all the people ran to see the sight
rich to be seen	Of hir array, so richely biseye;	Of their array, resplendent as they were;
at first	And than at erst amonges hem thay seye	And soon the common thought was whispered there,
he pleased	That Walter was no fool, though that hem leste	That Walter was no fool for being glad
	To chaunge his wyf; for it was for the beste.	To change his wife—a good exchange he had!
deem	For sche is fairer, as thay demen alle,	For she is fairer, as they notice all,
younger	Than is Grisild, and more tendre of age.	Than is Griselda, tenderer of age.

And the throngs of admiring serfs stood making their light remarks, forgetful of the victim of it all, and her undeserved disgrace. They watch the fair bride and the handsome boy beside her, and every moment the marquis seems to get more popular.

unsteady	O stormy poeple, unsad and ever untrewe,	O stormy people, light, and ever untrue,
indiscreet	And undiscret and chaunging as a fane,	And undiscerning—changing as a fane,
noise	Delytyng ever in rombel that is newe,	Delighting in new noise, because 'tis new,
	For lik the moone ay waxe ye and wane,	How like the moon do ye, too, wax and wane!
chattering	Ay ful of clappyng, dere ynough a jane, *	Your empty praise, like worthless coin, is vain:
judgment, ill proveth	Youre doom is fals, your constaunce yvil previth,	False is your judgment, frail your constancy,
believeth	A ful gret fool is he that on yow leevith.	Who trusts to you—a full great fool is he.

That is what the graver people in the city said when the populace were gazing up and down, glad for the novelty, to have a new lady in the castle.

Meanwhile Griselda was working busily at everything that was needed for the feast. She was nothing abashed at her clothing, though it was rude and coarse, and somewhat torn besides. She went to the gate with the rest to salute the bride, and hurried back at once to her work.

* "A jane is a small coin of Genoa (Janua); the meaning is, your praise is dear enough at a farthing."—B. Or the verse may be taken to mean, the smallest coin is dear enough to you when you are tired of better—for novelty's sake.

THE CLERK'S TALE

She received every one cheerfully, and in such a manner that no one had a fault to find with her; but some of them wondered who this woman was, in such shabby clothes, but who behaved with so much grace and propriety; and many praised her diligence and wisdom.

When all the great lords were about to sit down to supper, Walter called to Griselda, who was working in the hall.

GLOSSARY.		
do you like	Grisyld, quod he, as it were in his play, How likith the my wif and hir beauté?	"Grisild," he said to her, as if in play, "How seems my wife and her fair looks to thee?"
faith none	Right wel, my lord, quod sche, for in good fay A fairer saugh I never noon than sche. I pray to God yive hir prosperité; And so hope I that he wol to yow sende	"Right well, my lord," said she, "for in good fay I never saw a fairer bride than she; I pray God give you both prosperity; And so I hope that He will ever send
pleasantness	Plesaunce ynough unto your lyves ende.	You happiness enough to your lives' end.
beseech	On thing biseke I yow, and warne also, *	"One thing I pray of you, and warn beside,
prick	That ye ne prike with no tormentynge	That you goad not with any torturing
more (others)	This tendre mayden, as ye han doon mo:	This tender maid—like some you have sore tried
fostered, nourishing	For she is fostrid in hir norischinge	For she is nurtured in her upbringing
as I suppose	More tendrely, and to my supposyng:	More tenderly—and such a gentle thing
could, poorly	Sche couthe not adversité endure, As couthe a pore fostrid creature.	Might haply not adversity endure Like one whose nurture had been hard and poor."
	And whan this Walter saugh hir pacience, Hir glade cheer, and no malice at al, And he so oft hadde doon to hir offence,	And when this Walter saw her patientness, Her cheerful mien, and malice none at all; Though he so oft had tried her more or less,
steady	And sche ay sad, and constant as a wal, Continuyng ever hir innocence overal:	And she still firm and constant as a wall, Continuing ever her innocence over all:
direct	This sturdy marquis gan his herte dresse	This sturdy marquis 'gan his heart to chide,
to pity	To rewen upon hir wyfly stedefastnesse.	Touch'd by her steadfast faith that never died.
	This is ynough, Grisilde myn, quod he,	"This is enough, Griselda mine," said he,
afraid, disappointed	Be now no more agast, ne yvel apayed,	"Be no more ill at ease, and fear no more!
goodness	I have thy faith and thy benignité,	I have thy faith and strength and charity
essayed	As wel as ever womman was, assayed	Tempted, as woman never was before,
poorly	In gret estate, and pourliche† arrayed. Now knowe I, dere wyf, thy stedefastnesse.	Both in thy wealth, and in thy rags so poor. Now do I know, dear wife, thy steadfastness:"
kiss	And hir in armes took and gan hir kesse.	And clasp'd her in his arms with many a kiss.
heed	And sche for wonder took of it no keepe,	But she for wonder took no heed of him,

* Skeat; also second line beyond.   † Tyrwhitt and Skeat.

Glossary		
	Sche herde not what thing he to hir sayde,	She heard not any of the words he spoke,
fared, started	Sche ferd as sche hadde stert out of a sleepe,	She seemed as one that starteth from a dream
awoke	Til sche out of hir masidnesse abrayde.	Till she from her astonishment awoke.
died	Grisild, quod he, by God that for us deyde,	"Griselde," cried he, "it was a cruel joke:
	Thou art my wyf, non other I ne * have,	Thou art my wife, none other one I have,
	Ne never had, as God my soule save.	Nor ever had—as God my soul shall save!
	This is thy * doughter, which thou hast supposed	"This is thy daughter, whom thou hast supposed
	To be my wif: that other faithfully	To be my wife—that other faithfully
	Shal be myn heir, as I have ay purposed.	Shall be my heir, as I have long disposed;
	Thow bar hem of thy body trewely.	For they are both thy children, verily.
	At Boloyne have I kept hem prively.	I kept them at Bologna privily.
mayest thou	Tak hem agayn, for now maistow not seye	Take them again, thou canst not say, as once,
lost	That thou hast lorn noon of thy children tweye.	Thou hast lost either of thy little ones.
	And folk, that other weyes han seyd of me,	"And folk, who otherwise have said of me,
done	I warn hem wel, that I have doon this deede	I warn them well that I have acted thus,
	For no malice, ne for no crueltè,	Neither in malice nor in cruelty,
to assay, womanhood	But for tassaye in thee thy wommanhede;	Solely to prove thy patience marvellous,
forbid	And not to slen my children (God forbede!)	And not to slay my babes (God hinder us!)
quietly	But for to kepe hem prively and stille	But to conceal them secretly apart
	Til I thy purpos knewe, and al thy wille!	Until I learned thy purpose and thy heart!"

You may fancy you see Griselda at this moment, standing in her rags before the glittering company, and her brain dazed with wondering whether this were some new freak, or the truth that brought unheard-of joy. But nature had been taxed too far, and all her courage could not bear up against the shock.

in a swoon	Whan sche this herd, aswone doun she fallith,	When she heard this, all senseless down she falleth,
swooning	For pitous joy, and after her swownyng	For piteous joy—and half unconsciously
	Sche bothe hir yonge children to hir callith,	Both her young children unto her she calleth,
	And in hir armes, pitously wepyng,	And in her arms, weeping so piteously,
	Embraseth hem, and tendrely kissyng,	Embraceth them, with kisses tenderly,
tears	Ful lik a moder, with hir salte teres	Full like a mother, and the tears she sheds
their hair	Sche bathide bothe hir visage and hir heres.†	Bathe the fair faces and the dear loved heads.

Piteous it was to hear her humble voice, thanking Walter so fervently. "*Graunt mercy*, lord, God

---

* Tyrwhitt. † Skeat.

thank you," cried she, "for saving me my children. Now I care not how soon I die, since your love has come back to me.

Glossary.		
	O tendre, O dere, O yonge children myne, *	"O young, O dear, O tender children mine,
believed	Youre woful moder wende stedefastly	Your hapless mother thought in all her wo
wild dogs	That cruel houndes or som foul vermyne	That cruel beasts of prey and foul vermine
	Had eten yow: but God of his mercy,	Had slain you both; but God had mercy—lo!
	And your benigne fader tenderly	He and your loving father will'd it so
preserved you, moment	Hath doon yow kepe. And in that same stounde	That you should be preserved:" and said no more,
sank	Al sodeinly sche swapped doun to grounde.	But suddenly fell fainting on the floor.
swoon, firmly	And in hir swough so sadly holdith sche	And in her swoon so closely holdeth she
to embrace them	Hir children tuo, whan sche gan hem tembrace,	Her new-found children in a strong embrace.
skill	That with gret sleight and gret difficulté	That those around unclasp not easily
tear away	The children from her arm they gonne arace.	The fingers which so firmly interlace:
	O! many a teer on many a pitous face	O! many a tear on many a pitying face
down, stood, beside	Doun ran of hem that stooden hir bisyde,	Ran down in token of deep sympathy—
hardly	Unnethe aboute hir mighte thay abyde.	Scarce could they bear to watch her agony.
cheers, sorrow	Waltier hir gladith, and hir sorwe slakith,	Walter consoleth her as she awaketh:
abashed	Sche rysith up abaisshed from hir traunce,	She riseth up bewildered from her trance:
everybody	And every wight hir joy and feste makith,	Each presseth round about and merry maketh
countenance	Til sche hath caught agayn hir continaunce;	Until she hath recovered countenance.
comforts her	Wauter hir doth so faithfully plesaunce,	With kisses and with loving word and glance
dainty	That it was daynté for to see the cheere	Walter doth cheer her—sweet it was to see
company	Bitwix hem tuo, now thay be met in feere.	The joy they felt—united happily.
their, saw	These ladys, whan that thay hir tyme save,	And when they saw their time, these ladies gay
have	Han taken hir, and into chambre goon,	Unto a chamber led her forth with them,
	And strippen hir out of hir rude arraye,	And stript her out of all her rude array,
shone	And in a cloth of gold that brighte schon,	And in apparel bright with many a gem
crown, stone	With a coroun of many a riche stoon	Clad her, and, crownëd with a diadem
	Upon hir heed, they into hallo hir broughte,	Upon her head, they brought her to the hall,
she ought to be	And ther sche was honoured as hir oughte.	Where she was meetly honoured of them all.
	Thus hath this pitous day a blisful ende;	Thus hath this piteous day a blissful end,
best	For every man and womman doth his might	Till every man and woman in the rout
	This day in mirth and revel to despende,	Striveth the day in mirth and glee to spend,
welkin	Til on the welken schon the sterres brighte;	Till in the darken'd sky the stars shone out;

* Skeat and Tyrwhitt.

Glossary		
stately, man's	For more solempne in every mannes sighte	For greater and more sumptuous, without doubt,
greater, cost	This feste was, and gretter of costage,	This revel was—and there was more to pay—
	Than was the revel of hir mariage.	Than the rejoicings on her marriage-day.

Thus dwelt, for many years after, Walter and his wife in peace and joy; and I hope that the suffering of that day was the last Griselda had to bear at the hands of her capricious and wilful spouse. The pretty daughter Walter married to one of the greatest lords in Italy; and he then brought Griselda's old father to dwell in peace and comfort in his own court.

His son succeeded to his state and rank, and married happily, though he did not tempt and torment his wife as Walter did; for the world is not so strong as it once was, and people cannot bear such treatment now!

The story is told, not that wives should imitate Griselda in humility, for it would be unbearable, even if they did; but that every one in his degree should be constant in adversity as Griselda was. For if one woman could be so submissive to a mortal man, how much more ought we to take patiently all that God sends as our lot in life.

But one word before I stop! It would be hard to find in a whole city three, or even two, Griseldas nowadays. The gold in their nature is now so mixed with base metal that in any great trial the coin would sooner break than bend.

also	Grisild is deed, and eek hir pacience,	Dead is Griselda, and her patience,
once	And bothe at oones buried in Itayle;	Both buried in one grave in Italy;
	For whiche I crye in open audience	So I entreat in open audience
	No weddid man so hardy be to assayle	No wedded man be rash enough to try
	His wyves pacience, in hope to fynde	His own wife's patience, in the hope to find
	Grisildes, for in certeyn he schal fayle.	Griselda's, for he'll fail most certainly!

Notes by the Way.

The tender pathos in Chaucer's telling of this story (which he borrowed from Petrarch, but which is really much older than his time), cannot be excelled in any story we know of. The definite human interest running all through it points to some living Griselda, but who she was, or where she came from, no one knows. Resignation, so steadfast and so willing, was the virtue of an early time, when the husband was really a 'lord and master'; and such submission in a woman of the present civilization would be rather mischievous than meritorious. If a modern wife cheerfully consented to the murder of her children by her spouse, she would probably be consigned to a maison de santé, while her husband expiated his sins on the scaffold; and if she endured other persecutions, such as Griselda did, it is to be hoped some benevolent outsider would step in, if only to prevent cruelty to animals.

But it must be remembered that in the old world wives held a very different position in society, and the obedience of all the household to the lord of the castle was the chief secret of peace, discipline, and unity, as obedience to the captain of a vessel is now. We may also infer, from many hints in this Tale, the admiration felt for that kind of self-command in which people of a ruder time were so deficient. When almost everybody gave way habitually to violent emotions of all sorts, those who could rein in eeling were held in high esteem. Perhaps Walter himself may not have been wantonly cruel, but only so bewildered by these unaccustomed virtues that he could not trust their sincerity without experiments. *

Chaucer seems to me to have devoted especial pains to the Clerk's Tale, relating it in the same careful versification as the history of the pious Constance (Man of Law's Tale), the holy St. Cecilia (second Nonne's Tale), and the Prioress's Tale—all religious, and undoubtedly written *con amore*.

The story of Griselda winds up with real artistic power, the Clerk concluding with an ironical little song addressed to ordinary wives, so as to leave his hearers laughing, instead of depressed by the inadequate reward of patient Grizel's virtues. This little song consists of six beautiful verses, of six lines only each, and in which every line rhymes with the corresponding line in the five other verses. Clearly great labour has been lavished on it—but I have not included it, as the ironical directions to wives to be *bad* wives would be probably not understood by a child, and superfluous if they were.

---

* For the analysis of these two remarkable and elaborately worked-out characters, see *Chaucer for Schools*, p. 111.

𝕿𝖍𝖊 𝕱𝖗𝖆𝖓𝖐𝖑𝖎𝖓'𝖘 𝕿𝖆𝖑𝖊.

MINE host would not suffer long delay between the stories; and as soon as the last story was at an end, he called upon the Franklin to begin.

IN Armorike, * that is called Brittany, there was a knight named Arviragus, who loved the lady Dorigene. Much he laboured, and many a brave deed he performed for her sake. He loved her so dearly that no trouble seemed to him too great to win her love, for she was the fairest lady under the sun, and, moreover, came of high lineage. But, at last, seeing his worthiness and meek obedience, she consented to take him for her husband and her lord (such lordship as men have over their wives); and, in order that they might live more happily together, Arviragus, of his own free will, swore, as a knight, that he would never tyrannize over her, but follow her wishes in all things, as he had done ever.†

This kindness touched the lady deeply, and she thanked Arviragus; and, with great humility, she said, "Since of your gentillesse you proffer me so much power, I will always be a humble and true wife to you. Have here my troth, until my life shall end."

Thus they lived happily and at peace; for those who would live long together must give in to each other.

G<small>LOSSARY</small>.

mastery	Love wol nought ben constreigned by maystrie:	Love will not be constrained by tyranny;
soon	Whan maystrie cometh, the god of love anon	When mastery cometh, the god of Love anon
	Beteth his winges, and fare wel—he is gon!	Beateth his wings, and farewell!—he is gone!

For women wish for liberty, and not to be kept like slaves—and so do men also, if I tell truth. And whoever is patient in love, has all the advantage. Patience is a high virtue, for it overcomes things that rigour cannot do.

Arviragus went home with his wife to his own country, not far from Penmark,‡ where they dwelt 'in bliss and in solace.'

* Basse Bretaigne in France, called anciently Britannia Armorica.

† See Notes to this tale, p. 91, touching the homage paid to women during the middle ages.

‡ Penmark is placed on the maps on the western coast of Brittany, between Brest and Port l'Orient.

THE FRANKLIN'S TALE

When a year had passed away, this knight Arviragus made ready to go to England * to seek fame and honour in the service of arms, and there he dwelt two years.

But Dorigene loved her husband so dearly that she wept and fell sick when she was left alone. She could not sleep or eat, and as time went on, all her friends thought she would die. They tried to amuse her all that they could. Night and day they strove to comfort her, she was so sad, and begged her to go and roam with them in the fields and on the sea-shore.

You know even a stone will show some pattern at last if you cut long enough at it: and after a while Dorigene began to try and cheer up a little. Meanwhile, Arviragus sent letters home to tell her he would speedily return, else grief had slain her heart!

Now, Dorigene's castle stood near the sea; and sometimes she used to walk with her friends and her people on the cliffs, from whence she could see ever so many great ships and barges sailing by. But even the sea began to make her sad, for she said to herself, "Of all these ships that I see, is there not one will bring me back my lord?"

At other times she would sit and look down from the brink of the cliff; but when she saw the grisly black rocks that wrecked so many ships, her heart quaked with fear, and she sank on the green grass, and cried, with deep sighs of grief, "Would to God that all these black rocks were sunk into the earth, for my lord's sake!" and the piteous tears fell from her eyes.

Her friends soon saw it did her no good looking at the sea, but only made her worse. So they led her by rivers, and in beautiful green places, where they danced, and played at chess and tables. †

GLOSSARY.

morning	So on a day, right in the morwe tyde,	So on a day, before the sun was high,
	Unto a gardyne that was ther besyde,	Unto a garden fair that was hard by
	In which that thay hadde made here ordinaunce	(Wherein they had spread forth their meat and drink,
victual	Of vitaile, and of other purvyaunce,	And every comfort that the heart could think),
go, play	They gon and pleyen hem al the longe day.	They went—and sported all the whole long day,
	And this was on the sixte morwe of May, ‡	And this was on the sixth sweet morn of May,
	Which May had peynted with his softe schoures	When May had painted, with his tender showers,
	This gardyn ful of leves and of floures.	This garden full of fragrant leaves and flowers.

The odour of flowers and the fresh scene would have made any heart light that ever was born except one burdened by great sickness or great sorrow. After dinner they began to dance and sing—all save Dorigene, whose heart was sad. He whom she loved best was not among them.

There danced, among others, a squire before Dorigene, who was handsomer, and more radiant in array, and fresher than a May morning. He sang and danced better than anybody ever danced before, or will again! And, besides, he was young, strong, and virtuous, and rich and wise, and held in great esteem.

This squire, whose name was Aurelius, had long loved the Lady Dorigene, but she knew nothing of

---

* The only means of subsistence a knight had was fighting—of course for hire.

† Backgammon.

‡ About the 20th of May by our almanac.

it. He did not dare to tell her his grief, and could only sing songs, in which he complained in a general way that he loved some one who regarded him not.

He made a great many songs in this strain.

But at last, on this day it happened, as Aurelius was her neighbour, and a man of worship and honour, Dorigene fell a-talking with him; and when he saw a chance, Aurelius said to her, "Madam, I wish when Arviragus went over the sea, I had gone whither I could never come back! For well I know you do not care for me. Madam, forget Arviragus: and love me a little, or I shall die!"

Dorigene looked at him, and said, "Is this your will? I never knew what you meant. But now, this is my answer: I cannot forget my Arviragus, and I do not care for any one but him!"

But afterwards she said in play, "Aurelius, I will love you when you have taken away all the rocks and stones that hinder the ships from sailing. And when you have made the coast so clear that there is not a single stone to be seen, then I will love you best of any man." For she well knew the rocks could never be moved.

But Aurelius was sorely grieved. "Is there no other grace in you?" said he. "No, by that Lord who made me," Dorigene answered. "Madam, it is an impossibility," he said; "I must die."

Then came Dorigene's other friends, who knew nothing of this. They roamed up and down the green alleys, and betook themselves to new sports and new revels; but Aurelius did not mingle with them. He went sorrowfully to his own home, for it seemed as though he felt his heart grow cold.

He as so sad that he fell sick, and so suffered a long, long time, telling his trouble to nobody in the world; except to his brother, who was a clerk, * and who was very sorry for him.

GLOSSARY.

see	His breast was hole withouten for to sene,	His breast was whole without, to every eye,
ever	But in his herte ay was the arwe kene.	But in his heart the arrow keen did lie.

And well you know that it is a perilous cure when a wound is healed outwardly only!

Meanwhile, Arviragus came home from England to his faithful wife, and there were great rejoicings, and feasts, and joustings; and these two were so glad to see each other that they thought of nothing else. Dorigene cared nothing at all for Aurelius; and Arviragus had no suspicion that Aurelius had spoken to her of love.

Now Aurelius' brother was a very learned man; and as he saw Aurelius got no better, he was very unhappy about him. At last he remembered that he had once seen at Orleans, in France, a book on conjuring,† which had been left in his way. This book was full of all sorts of curious tricks which were performed by the 'tregetoures' or jugglers of that day. He was glad when he thought of this book, feeling sure he saw a chance of curing Aurelius.

	And whan this boke was in his remembraunce,	And when this book came, by a lucky chance,
immediately	Anon for joye his herte gan for to daunce,	Into his mind, his heart began to dance,

---

* *Clerk* at that time denoted a man of learning, and a student at the universities—generally in holy orders.

† *Natural Magic*, Chaucer.—All kinds of conjuring were very popular at this time. The minstrels or *jougleurs* added to their other accomplishments marvellous skill in sleight of hand (derived from the East): hence the modern signification of the word *juggler*. It is quite clear that many of their tricks were due to electro-biology, a science known to those mighty cultivators and preservers of learning, the Arabs. For some knowledge of what we owe to the Arabs, and of their influence upon mediæval European literature, I refer the reader to the 'Literary Remains of Emanuel Deutsch' (published by John Murray), containing two articles on Arabic Poetry; and to Draper's popular 'History of the Conflict between Religion and Science.'

DORIGEN AND AURELIUS IN THE GARDEN

'Have mercy, swete, or ye wol do me deye.'

THE FRANKLIN'S TALE

GLOSSARY.		
	And to him selve he sayde pryvely,	And to himself he whispered privily,
cured	My brother shal be warisshed hastely,	"My brother shall be healed full speedily,
sure	For I am siker that ther ben sciences	For I am sure that there be sciences
various	By whiche men maken dyverse apparences,	By which men raise divers appearances,
	Swiche as thise subtile tregetoures pleyen,	Such as the cunning jugglers do in play;
	For oft at festes have I wel herde seyen	For oftentimes at feasts have I heard say
	That tregettoures withinne an halle large	That jugglers playing in a hall so large,
	Han made come in a water and a barge,	Have seemed to bring in waters and a barge,
	And in the halle rowen up and doun.	And in the hall they row it to and fro.
seemed, grim	Sometyme hath semed come a grym leoun,	Sometimes a lion fierce will come and go,
	And sometyme floures spring as in a mede, *	Sometimes, as in a meadow, flowers upspring,
	Sometyme a vine, and grapes white and rede,	Sometimes a vine, with rich fruit clustering,
	Sometyme a castel al of lym and ston,	Sometimes a castle all of lime and stone,
dispersed	And whan hem liked voyded it anon.	And when they wish, at once the whole is gone!
	Thus semeth it to every mannes sight.	Thus seemeth it to be, in all men's sight."

Therefore he thought that if he could find any old friend at Orleans, who knew anything of magic, he might help Aurelius to win the beautiful Dorigene.

He went to his brother's bed, and gave him so much hope that he sprang up at once and started off to Orleans.

When they were nearly arrived at the city, they met a young clerk, roaming by himself, who greeted them in Latin, saying, to their great wonder, "I know the cause that brings you here," and, ere they went a step farther, he told them all that was in their minds!

This clerk was, you see, a magician, and having saved them the trouble of explaining their business, he brought them to his house, where he feasted them in splendid style, and showed them many wonderful visions.

supper	He schewed hem, er they went to soupere,	He made appear, before they went to meat,
	Forestes, parkes, full of wilde dere;	Forests and parks, with wild deer fair and fleet;
	There † saw he hartes with hir hornes hie,	There saw he harts that tossed their antlers high,
	The gretest that were ever seen with eie!	The greatest that were ever seen with eye!
	He saw of hem an hundred slain with houndes,	He saw a hundred of them slain by hounds,
	And som with arwes blede of bitter woundes.	While some with arrows bled of bitter wounds,
departed	He saw, when voided were the wilde dere,	And when the wild deer were no longer there,
	Thise faukoneres upon a faire rivere,	Came falconers upon a river fair,
hawks	That with hir haukes han the heron slein.	Who, with their falcons, have the heron slain;
joust	Tho saw he knyhtes justen in a pleyn;	Then saw he knights all jousting in a plain;

---

* This and the following line are not in Morris's edition.

† Bell's edition. This and the next six lines are not in Morris's edition.

Glossary.	And after this he dide him such plesaunce,	And after this he gave him such pleasance,
	That he him schewed his lady in a daunce,	That he could see his lady in a dance,
	On which himself he dauncéd, as him thouht.	In which himself was dancing, as he thought.
	And when this mayster that this magique wrouht,	And when this master, who the magic wrought,
two	Sawh it was tyme, he clapped his hondes tuo,	Saw it was time, he clapped his hands, and eh!
done	And, fare wel! al the revel is y-do!	Farewell! for all the revel fades away!
	And yet remued they never out of the hous	And yet they never moved from out the house,
	While they saw alle this sightes mervelous;	While they did see these visions marvellous;
	But in his studie, ther his bookes be,	But in his study, where his volumes lay,
	They saten stille, and no wighte but they thre.	They sat alone, and no man else but they.

Therefore, after all these wondrous sights, inside the magician's study, there was no doubt that he could make the rocks disappear on the coast of Brittany!

Aurelius asked him how much money he should give him to perform that feat, and the magician said he must have no less than a thousand pounds; * but Aurelius said he would give him the whole world if he could; and it was agreed that for this sum he should make the rocks vanish, and that without delay!

The next morning, at daybreak, Aurelius, his brother, and the magician, went to the sea-side of Brittany, where the feat was to be done: it was the cold frosty month of December.

Aurelius paid the magician every attention in his power, and entreated him to hasten to alleviate his misery; he rather ungraciously added, that he would slit his heart with his sword if he didn't.

The cunning sorcerer made as much haste as he could with his spells and trickeries to make all the rocks sink, or seem to sink, before the eyes of all that looked at them, right underground; at last he succeeded. By his magic arts it really did seem to everybody, for a week or two, that the rocks were all gone.

Aurelius thanked him with joy, and then hastened to the castle, where he knew he should see Dorigene, to remind her of what she had promised.

"My sovereign lady," he said, saluting her humbly—

promised	Ye wot right wel what ye byhighte me,	"You know right well what you have promised me,
my	And in myn hond your trouthe plighte ye	And hand in mine your fair trouth plighted ye
	To love me best; God woot ye sayde so,	To love me best; God knoweth you said so,
	Al be that I unworthy am therto.	Although I be unworthy thereunto.
you	Madame, I speke it for thonour of yow	Madam, I speak for th' honour of the vow
	More than to save myn hertes lif right now:	More than to urge my heart's deep longing now:
	I have do so as ye comaundede me,	For I have done as you commanded me,
vouchsafe	And if ye vouchesauf ye maye go se.	And if you please it, you may go and see.
lieth	In yow lith al to do me lyve or deye,	It rests with you, to let me live or die,
are	But wel I wote the rokkes ben aweye.	But that the rocks have vanish'd, well know I."

* Equal to eight or ten times the amount now.

Poor Dorigene had little expected to fall into such a trap! She stood astonished, and her face grew white—all the colour left her cheeks. How bitterly she repented her rash promise! for she did not want to go away with Aurelius. "Alas!" she cried, "that such a thing should be! how could I guess so monstrous a marvel could come to pass?" and her terror made her like one desperate.

Her husband, Arviragus, too, was absent, and there was no one she could tell her trouble to. She cried and lamented for three days, vainly thinking how she could get out of the scrape; and at last she determined to die. So three days passed, and all the time she was weeping and resolving on her death.

However, on the third night, Arviragus came home again; and, when he knew what she was weeping so bitterly for, he said, cheerfully and kindly, "Is that all, Dorigene?"

GLOSSARY.

else	Is ther aught elles, Dorigen, but this?	"Is there aught further, Dorigene, than this?"
reads, knows	Nay, nay, quod sche, God me so rede and wis	"Nay, nay," cried she, "God help me, for it is
if	This is to moche, and it were Goddes wille!	Too much already—were it but His will!"
	Ye, wyf, quod he, let slepe that may be stille, *	"Yea, wife," he answered, "what has been is still,
peradventure	It may be wel, paraunter, yet to-day.	But yet, perchance, it may be well to-day.
faith	Ye schal your trouthe holden, by my fay,	That promise you shall hold to, by my fay,
wisely	For God so wisly have mercy on me,	For as I hope for mercy from on high,
rather, slain	I hadde wel lever i-stekid for to be,	I would more willingly consent to die,
	For verray love which that I to you have,	Yea for the love's sake that I bear to you,
unless	But if ye scholde your trouthe kepe and save,	Than you should break the honour of a vow
	Trouthe is the hiest thing that man may kepe.	Faith is the highest thing that can be kept."
burst	And with that word he brast anon to wepe.	And with that word he broke away and wept.

Poor Arviragus, this brave and just knight, bade Dorigene keep her word at any cost to herself or him, but he could not keep up his cheerful tone. He was too deeply grieved and hurt, and even wept with her for sorrow.

Then he commanded a squire and a maid to attend Dorigene for a part of the way to the garden, where Aurelius would fetch her.

Now, Aurelius happened to meet her on her way to the garden, in one of the busiest streets of the town. He saluted her joyfully, and asked her whither she was going. But Dorigene was distracted with grief.

And sche answered, half as sche were mad,	And she made answer half as she were mad,
Unto the gardyn, as myn housbond bad,	"Unto the garden, as my husband bade,
My trouthe for to holde, allas! allas!	To keep my troth to you, alas! alas!"

When Aurelius heard that, he was deeply touched that Arviragus should have sent her, weeping as she was, rather than she should break her promise. See how proud and how strong the sense of honour was in those days! He felt that after such a sacrifice he would rather forego everything than insist upon his right to take away Dorigene, which, he felt, would be *'churlish wretchedness against fraunchise of all gentillesse'* †—a deed against courtesy and honour. And he said, "Madam, say to your lord, Arviragus, that

---

* Equivalent to 'What is done cannot be undone.'   † I could not resist inserting the vigorous old words.

since I see he would rather suffer anything than that you should fail in truth, and since I see that you care far more for Arviragus than ever you will for me—even if you went away with me, you would never love me as much as Arviragus—I would rather be unhappy all my life than make you so. I release you from your promise for ever."

G<small>LOSSARY</small>.

do	Thus can a squyer doon a gentil dede,	Thus can a squire do a noble deed
	As wel as can a knyghte, withouten drede.	As nobly as a knight can, without dread.

Dorigene fell down on her knees and thanked him, and went back to her husband happy, and they lived in bliss ever after.

Aurelius, however, though his conscience was clear, bethought him of all his trouble and the money he had spent to no purpose. He had willingly promised all his fortune when he thought he could win beautiful Dorigene; but now he said, "I must sell my heritage, but I cannot live here a beggar to shame my kindred; unless the magician would be so kind as to let me pay the thousand pounds little by little. I will not break my promise to him. He shall have the money though I have got nothing by it."

sore	With herte soor he goth unto his cofre,	With mournful heart he went unto his coffer
philosopher	And broughte gold unto this philosophre,	And took such gold as he was free to offer,
	The value of fyf hundred pound, I gesse,	The value of five hundred pounds, I guess;
beseecheth	And him bysecheth of his gentillesce,	Beseeching him, of his kindheartedness,
remnant	To graunte him dayes of the remenaunt;	To grant him for the rest some time to pay,
boast	And sayde, Maister, I dar wel make avaunt	And said, "Master, I do not fear to say
	I fayled never of my trouthe as yit,	I never failed to keep my word as yet;
surely	For sikerly my dettes schall be quyt	Truly my debt to you I shall acquit,
	Towardes yow, how so that ever I fare	Whatever comes—though I must needs at best
beg, tunic	To goon and begge in my kurtil bare,	Go begging in my shirt to find the rest.
vouchsafe, surety	But wolde ye vouchesauf upon seurté,	But would ye grant, on good security,
	Tuo yere or thre for to respite me,	To give me credit for two years, or three,
	Than were I wel, for elles most I selle	Then all were well, for else I must needs sell
	Myn heritage, ther is nomore to telle.	My heritage—there is no more to tell."

The magician soberly answered, "Did I not keep my covenant with you?"

"Yes, well and truly," said Aurelius.

"And did you not take the lady away with you?"

"No, no," said Aurelius, sadly; and he told him all that had happened.

The magician answered, "Dear friend, every one of you has behaved honourably. Thou art a squire, and he is a knight, but a simple clerk can do a gentle deed, as well as any of you! Sir, I release you from your thousand pounds: I will not take a penny from you." And he took his horse and rode away.

Chaucer winds up by saying—

ask	Lordynges, this questioun wold I axe now—ask	Masters, a little question answer me—
liberal	Which was the moste free, as thinketh yow?	Which one was the most generous of the three?

And you, tell me which you think was the most honourable in keeping faith, and most generous in giving up his rights.

But beware of the folly that Dorigene committed, in making rash promises; for when you make a promise you must be prepared to keep it, and cannot always expect to be let off as she was.

Notes by the Way.

One of the most interesting illustrations of the singular morality which was the outcome of woman's transition state from a position of slavery to one of equality with man, is to be found in this curious but beautiful tale: a tale which in any other age could scarcely have been popular. The Franklin tells us it was an old Breton lay; which, however, is now not known to exist.

It is seen that woman, from being regarded as a mere chattel, like horse or dog, came to be unnaturally exalted; and, as new movements often outshoot their mark and go too far, she came to be held as something god-like and ideal, the moving spring of all heroic virtues. Valour, courtesy, self-control, obedience, were taught by her, and she could give no higher guerdon than herself. (See note to 'Knight's Tale,' p. 45.)

It is the young and inexperienced hound which outruns the scent, not the fully trained dog, and we must remember that society had then the virtues and vices of immaturity. The Franklin's Tale, with its pathos and earnestness, passing at times into burlesque, is as quaint and instructive as an early effigy on some cathedral door.

A certain soft and refined luxuriousness seems to hang like a gossamer veil over a sentiment of genuine and vigorous chivalry, carried too far for our 19th century notions, but, like the generous mistakes of youth, none the less touching.

The moral of this striking tale points out the danger of giving even the smallest inlet to wrong dealing; since a condition apparently impossible to realize may after all work our ruin.

The Pardoner's Tale.

THEN mine host turned to the Pardoner: "Thou, pardoner, thou, my good friend," he said—

Tel us a tale, for thou canst many oon.	"Tell us a tale; thou knowest many an one."
It schal be doon, quod he, and that anoon.	"I will!" he said; "it shall at once be done.
But first, quod he, her at this ale-stake *	But first," he added, "here at this ale-stake
I wil bothe drynke and byten on a cake.	I'll take a drink, and have a bite of cake."

When he had done so (for they were passing a roadside inn), he began, as you shall hear:—

THERE was in Flanders a company of young folk, who gave themselves up to folly and wrong-doing. They did nothing but gamble and riot, and drink wine, and dance, and swear; and their gluttony and idleness made them wicked, so that when they heard of other people committing sin they laughed and did as much wrong as ever they could.

This kind of life degrades every one. Gluttony was the first cause of our confusion: Adam and Eve were driven from Paradise for that vice. And drunkenness leads to many other sins, as is shown in Holy Writ.

Three of these bad young men were sitting in a tavern one morning very early, drinking, when they heard the clinking of a bell † before a corpse that was being carried to the grave. One of them called to his boy, "Go out, and ask who that dead man is who passes by; and mind you bring his name back right!"

"Master," said the boy, "there is no need to go and ask, for I heard who the dead man was two hours before you came into this tavern. He was one of your own companions, and he was slain last night as he sat in his chair drinking, by a privy thief named Death, who kills everybody in this country. With his spear he smote his heart in two, and went away without speaking. About a thousand has he

---

* The ale-stake was a stake set up as a sign before the inn, generally adorned with a bush. This custom prevails in Normandy still, where you may see a goodly bunch of mistletoe hanging out wherever wine or cider is sold.

† "A small bell used formerly to be rung before the corpse as it was carried to the grave, to give notice to those who were charitably disposed that they might pray for the soul of the deceased. Our 'passing bell' has the same origin, though the reason for it has ceased."—*Bell.*

killed this pestilence. * And, master, it seems to me, that before he comes to you too, it were as well to be prepared. Beware of him, be ready for him! my dame ever taught me that."

G<small>LOSSARY</small>.

innkeeper	By seinte Mary, sayde this taverner,	"By holy Mary," said the innkeeper,
true	The child saith soth, for he hath slayn this yeer,	"The child says true, for he hath slain this year,
	Hens over a myle, withinne a gret village,	Within a mile hence, in a large village,
labourer	Bothe man and womman, child, and hyne, and page.	Both man and woman, servant, child, and page.

"I should think he lived there, this Death, so many have died. It were wise to be warned before he came suddenly on a man!"

"Good lack," cried one of the rioters with an oath, "is it then such danger to meet him? I'll seek him out by street and stile.

hearken, be	Herkneth, felaws, we thre ben all oones,	"Now listen, mates, for all we three are one,
hand	Let ech of us hold up his hond † to other,	Let each hold up his hand unto the other,
	And ech of us bycome otheres brother;	And each of us become the others' brother.
	And we wil slee this false traitour Deth;	And we will slay this sneaking traitor Death,
slain, slayeth	He shall be slayne, that so many sleeth.	He shall be slain, he that so many slay'th."

So these three men, half drunk as they were, plighted faith to live and die for each other, as though they were brothers born. And up they started, and went forth to this village, of which the innkeeper had spoken, where they thought Death lived. And much bad language they used, and many wicked things they said, resolving to catch Death before night fell.

turned	Right as thay wolde han torned over a style,	Just as they were about to cross a stile,
	Whan thai han goon nought fully half a myle,	When they had gone not fully half a mile,
	An old man and a pore with hem mette.	A poor and aged man did meet them there.
meekly, greeted	This olde man ful mekely hem grette, ‡	This old man greeted them with civil air,
God see you	And saide thus, Lordynges, God yow se!	And said, "Good day, my lords, God look on ye."
rioters	The proudest of these ryotoures thre	Then the most arrogant of the noisy three
churl	Answerd ayein, What, carle, with sory grace,	Answered him thus—"What, churl, with sorry grace,
wrapped up	Why artow al for-wrapped save thi face? §—	Why art thou all wrapped up except thy face?

* "Perhaps an allusion to the great pestilence which devastated Europe during the 14th century. *This pestilence* means *during* this pestilence, as *this year* means *during* this year."—*Bell*.

† "This is still the ceremony used in taking an oath in courts of justice in Prussia."—*Bell*. Notice the emphasis laid on their close friendship, and their constant allusion to their being all 'one,' over and above the solemnity of the profane vow they make.

‡ The kindly custom of greeting passers-by, now rapidly going out even in our country districts, was more common in days when passers-by were infinitely rarer. Probably half a mile from the inn the road was lonesome enough, wherefore the old man's anticipation of rough treatment from three reckless and half-tipsy ruffians was not unreasonable. His calm and fearless answer was the wisest as well as the most dignified course to pursue with such assailants, being calculated to sober them as well as to save himself.

§ Making a jest of the close coverings and wraps of old age.

	Why lyvest thou longe in so great an age?
began, look	This olde man gan loke on his visage,
because	And saide thus: For that I can not fynde
	A man—though that I walke into Inde—
	Neither in cité noon, ne in village,
	That wol chaunge his youthe for myn age;
	And therfore moot I have myn age stille
	As longe tyme as it is Goddes wille,
	Ne Deth, allas! ne wil not have my lif,
	Thus walk I lik a resteles caytif, *
	And on the ground, which is my modres gate,
	I knokke with my staf, erly and late,
dear	And saye, Leeve moder, let me in.
	Lo, how I wane, fleisch, and blood, and skyn—
shall, bones	Allas, whan schuln my boones ben at rest?
	Moder, with yow wil I chaunge my chest,
	That in my chamber longe tyme hath be,
enwrap	Ye, for an haire clout † to wrap-in me.
favour	But, yet to me sche wol not do that grace,
withered	For which ful pale and welkid is my face.
	But sires, to yow it is no curtesye
	To speke unto an old man vilonye,
unless, else	But he trespas in word or elles in dede.
read	In holy writ ye may yourself wel rede,
in presence of	Ayens an old man, hoor upon his hede,
exhort	Ye schold arise: wherefor I you rede
do not	Ne doth unto an old man more harm now,
	Namore than ye wolde men dede to yow
live so long	In age, if that ye may so long abyde.
walk	And God be with you, wherso ye go or ryde!
thither	I moot go thider as I have to goo.
	Nay, olde cherl, by God thou shalt not so,

Why livest thou so long, and art so grey?"
The old man looked him in the face straightway,
And answer'd thus: "Because I cannot find
A man—e'en though I walk'd as far as Inde—
Neither in any city, nor villàge,
Willing to change his youth for mine old age;
And therefore must I have my old age still
As long a time as it is heaven's will.
Nor will e'en Death receive my life, alas!
Thus like a restless wayfarer I pass,
And on the ground, which is my mother's gate,
Keep knocking with my staff early and late,
And say to her—'Dear mother, let me in.
Lo, how I vanish, flesh and blood and skin—
Alas, when shall my bones remain at rest?
Mother, I want to change with you my chest,
Which in my room so long a time hath been,
Yea, for a cloth of hair to wrap me in!'
But yet to me she will not do that grace,
Wherefore so pale and wrinkled is my face.

"But, sirs, in you it is no courtesy
To speak to an old man disdainfully,
Unless he shall offend in word or deed.
In Holy Writ ye may your own selves read,
Before an aged man whose hair is grey
Ye should rise up—and therefore I you pray
Offer to an old man no mischief now
More than you would that men did unto you
In your old age, if you so long abide,
And God be with you, whither you walk or ride!
I must go on, whither I have to go."

"Nay, thou old churl, thou shalt not quit us so."

---

* *Caitif*, wretch, wretched. Italian—*cattivo*, captive. Fr.—*chétif*, poor, wretched, paltry, pitiful, &c. *Captive* seems to give the most pathetic meaning, as though death were a looked-for freedom by a restless prisoner in the body. Fugitive is the next best for the sense, as the old man may be supposed to be flying to the gate for safety and comfort.

† Hair-shroud, sackcloth, the roughest cloth.

THE PARDONER'S TALE

GLOSSARY.		
departest, easily }	Sayde that other hasardour anoon,	Cried out the other rioter anon,
	Thou partist nought so lightly, by seint Johan!	"Thou partest not so lightly, by St. John!
	Thou spak right now of thilke traitour Deth,	Thou hast just spoken of that traitor Death
	That in this contré alle our frendes sleth;	Who all our friends through all the country slay'th,
here	Have her my trouth, as thou art his aspye;	So now I warrant thee, thou art his spy;
	Tel wher he is, or elles thou schalt dye. *	Tell where he is, this Death, or thou shall die.

"You needn't deny that you know of his whereabouts—for you are in his plot to get rid of us young folks, you wretched old thief!"

	Now, sires, than if that yow be so leef	"Now, sirs," quoth he, "if you so eager be
	To fynde Deth, torn up this croked way,	To seek for Death, turn up this crooked way,
	For in that grove I laft him, † by my fay,	For in that grove I left him, by my fay,
remain	Under a tree, and ther he wil abyde.	Under a tree, and there he will abide,
boast	Ne for your bost he nyl him no thing hyde.	Nor for your noise and boasting will he hide.
	Se ye that ook? right ther ye schuln him fynde.	See ye that oak? close there his place you'll find,
again	God save yow, that bought agein mankynde,	God save you, sirs, that hath redeem'd mankind,
	And yow amend. Thus sayth this olde man,	And mend you all"—thus said the aged man.
every one	And everich of these riotoures ran,	And thereupon each of the rioters ran
	Til thay come to the tre, and ther thay founde	Until they reach'd the tree, and there they found
coined	Of florins fyn of gold ycoyned rounde,	A heap of golden florins, bright and round,
	Wel neygh a seven busshels, as hem thoughte.	Well-nigh seven bushels of them, as they thought.
	No lenger thanne after Deth thay soughte,	And then no longer after Death they sought,
	But ech of hem so glad was of that sighte,	But each of them so glad was at the sight,
	For that the florens so faire were and brighte,	The florins were so beauteous and so bright,
	That doun thai sette hem by the precious hord.	That down they sat beside the precious hoard.
	The werste ‡ of hem he spake the firste word.	The worst one was the first to speak a word.
	Bretheren, quod he, take kepe what I schal saye,	"Brothers," said he, "take heed of what I say,
wisdom, jest }	My witte is gret, though that I bourde and playe,	For I am wise, although I jest and play,
given	This tresour hath fortune to us yiven,	This treasure makes our fortune, so that we
jollity, live	In mirth and jolyté our lif to lyven,	May lead our lives in mirth and jollity,
cometh	And lightly as it comth, so wil we spende.	And lightly as it comes, we'll lightly spend.
supposed	Ey, Goddis precious dignite, who wende	By heaven! who would have thought that luck would send

* Tyrwhitt's edition has the less bloody threat, 'Tell wher he is, or thou shalt it abie!'

† The old man probably saw that the young men were scarcely responsible for their actions, and determined to wreak violence on some one, and therefore he played on their mood to avert their violence from himself to some other object.

‡ Tyrwhitt.

Glossary		
	Today, that we schuld have so fair a grace?	Us three good friends to-day so fair a grace?
	But mighte this gold be caried fro this place	But could this gold be carried from this place
	Hom to myn hous, or ellis unto youres,	Home to my house, or else to one of yours
know	(For wel I wot that this gold is nought oures),	(For all this gold I well know is not ours)
high	Than were we in heyh felicité.	Then were we in complete felicity.
	But trewely by day it may not be,	But, truly, during day it cannot be,
	Men wolde saye that we were theves stronge,	People would call us thieves, and possibly
have us hanged	And for our tresour doon us for to honge.	Hang us for our own treasure on a tree.
	This tresour moste caried be by nighte	This treasure should be carried off by night,
	As wysly and as slely as it mighte.	As cleverly and slily as it might.
advise	Wherfore I rede, that cut among us alle	I counsel then, that we among us all
	We drawe, and let se wher the cut wil falle,	Draw lots, and see to whom the lot will fall,
blithe heart	And he that hath the cut, with herte blithe,	And he that hath the lot shall cheerfully
run, quickly	Shal renne to the toun, and that ful swithe,	Go back into the town, and speedily,
	And bring us bred and wyn ful prively,	And bring us bread and wine full privily;
	And tuo of us shal kepe subtilly	Meanwhile we two keep safe and secretly
delay	This tresour wel: and if he wol not tarie,	This treasure here: and if he do not tarry,
	Whan it is night, we wol this tresour carie,*	When the night comes we will the treasure carry,
whither	By oon assent, ther as us liketh best.	By one assent, where we think best, or list."
fist	That oon of hem the cut brought in his fest,	This man then held the lots within his fist,
look	And bad hem drawe and loke wher it wil falle,	And bade them draw and see where it would fall;
	And it fel on the yongest of hem alle,	It fell upon the youngest of them all,
at once	And forth toward the toun he went anoon.	Who therefore toward the town went forth anon.
	And al so soone as that he was agoon,	As soon as their companion was gone
	That oon of hem spak thus unto that other:	The first one subtly spoke unto the other:
	Thou wost wel that thou art my sworne brother,	"Thou knowest well that thou art my sworn brother,
directly	Thy profyt wol I telle the anoon.	I'll tell thee what thy profit is to-day.
knowest	Thou wost wel that our felaw is agoon,	Thou seest that our fellow is away,
plenty	And her is gold, and that ful gret plente,	And here is gold, all heap'd up plenteously,
	That schal departed be among us thre.	Which is to be divided 'mong us three.
	But natheles if I can schape it so	But, nevertheless, if I can shape it so
	That it departed were betwix us tuo,	That it might be divided 'mong us *two*,
	Hadde I not doon a frendes torn to the?	Have I not done a friend's turn unto thee?"
know not	That other answerd, I not how that may be;	"I know not," said the other, "how that may be;

* Probably in the vessels, &c., which had contained the food, thus avoiding the appearance of transporting treasure.

THE RIOTER

'For this witterly was his ful entente—
To slen hem bothe, and never to repente.'

Glossary.		
two	He wot wel that the gold is with us twaye,	He knows quite well the gold is with us two,
say	What schulde we than do? what schulde we saye?	What should we say to him? what should we do?"
wicked person	Schal it be counsail? * sayd the ferste schrewe,	"Shall it be counsel?" said the first again—
	And I schal telle thee in wordes fewe	"And in a few words I shall tell thee plain,
do	What we schul doon, and bringe it wel aboute.	What we shall do to bring the thing about."
	I graunte, quod that other, without doute,	"I promise," said the other, "without doubt
betray	That by my trouthe I wil thee nought bywraye.	That I, for one, will not be treacherous."
knowest	Now, quoth the first, thou wost wel we ben twaye,	"Now," said the first one, "there are two of us,
	And two of us schal strenger be than oon.	And two of us will stronger be than one.
look	Loke, whanne he is sett, thou right anoon †	Look, thou, when he is sitting down, and soon
wouldest	Arys, as though thou woldest with him pleye, ‡	Rise up, as if to play with him, and I
rip	And I schal ryf him through the sydes tweye,	Will stab him through the two sides suddenly,
	Whils that thou strogelest with him as in game,	While thou art struggling with him as in game,
	And with thi dagger, loke thou do the same.	And with thy dagger, look, thou do the same.
divided	And than schal al the gold departed be,	And then shall all this gold divided be,
thee	My dere frend, bitwixe the and me:	My dearest friend, betwixt thyself and me:
might	Than may we oure lustes al fulfille,	Then all our wants and whims we can fulfil,
dice	And pley at dees right at our owne wille.	And play at dice according to our will."

Thus these two ruffians made their compact to murder the third, as I have described.

who	This yongest, which that wente to the toun,	The youngest, who had gone into the town,
close	Full fast in hert he rollith up and doun	Deep in his mind he turneth up and down
	The beaute of these florins, newe and brighte.	The beauty of these florins, new and bright.
	O Lord, quoth he, if so were that I mighte	"O Lord," quoth he, "if any-wise I might
	Have all this gold unto myself alloone,	Have all this treasure to myself alone,
throne	Ther is no man that lyveth under the troone	There is no man that dwelleth under the throne
	Of God, that schulde lyve so mery as I.	Of God, who then should live so merry as I."
	And atte last the feend, oure enemy,	And at the last the fiend, our enemy,
buy	Put in his thought that he schulde poysoun beye,	Put in his thought that he should poison buy,
slay	With which he mighte sle his felawes tweye.	With which to cause his comrades both to die.
	For why? the feend fond him in such lyvynge	For why? the fiend found this man's life so foul
sorrow	That he hadde leve to sorwe him to brynge:	That he had power now upon his soul:
	For this was outrely § his ful entente	For this was utterly his fix'd intent
slay	To slen hem bothe, and never to repente.	To slay them both and never to repent

* Shall counsel he kept between us? literally, in schoolboys' language, 'Mum's the word—eh?'   † Bell's edition.

‡ Games which we now leave to children were formerly as popular with grown-up people. Hunt-the-slipper and blind-man's-buff were 200 years ago the common recreation of ladies and gentlemen, and wrestling and other romping was indulged in far more commonly than now by young men. Playing at ball was a favourite pastime.

§ Tyrwhitt. *Outrely,* utterly, beyond all things.→

Glossary		
delay	And forth he goth, no lenger wold he tarye,	And forth he goes, no longer would he tarry,
apothecary	Into the toun unto a potecarye,	Into the town to an apothecary,
	And prayde him that he him wolde selle	And begged him plausibly that he would sell
rats	Som poysoun, that he might his rattis quelle;	Him poison strong enough the rats to quell;
farmyard	And eek ther was a polkat in his hawe	Also, there was a polecat in his yard
	That, as he sayde, his capouns had i-slawe,	Which had destroy'd his capons, he averr'd,
avenge	And said he wold him wreke, if that he mighte,	And he would gladly rid him if he might
	Of vermyn, that destroyed hem by nighte.	Of vermin, which destroy'd them in the night.
the apothecary	Thapotecary answerd, * Thou schalt have	The apothecary answered, "Thou shalt have
	A thing that, also God my soule save,	Something so strong, as God my soul shall save,
	In al this world ther nys no creature	That in this world nothing that living is
mixture	That ete or dronk hath of this confecture—	Who in his food doth eat or drink of this—
amount	Nought but the mountaunce of a corn of whete—	Nay, but the greatness of a grain of wheat—
quit	That he ne schuld his lif anoon for-lete;	Shall fail to die, his life shall be forfeit;
die	Ye, sterve he schal, and that in lasse while	Yea, he shall die, and that in lesser while
step	Than thou wilt goon a paas not but a myle,	Than thou shalt walk a step beyond a mile,
	This poysoun is so strong and violent.	This poison is so strong and violent."
caught or taken	This cursed man hath in his hond i-hent	This curséd man hath taken it and pent
then	This poysoun in a box, and sins he ran	The poison in a box, and forthwith ran
	Into the nexte stret unto a man	Hastily to the next street, to a man
	And borwed of him large boteles thre,	And borrow'd of him some large bottles three,
	And in the two his poysoun poured he:	And into two the poison pouréd he:
third, clean	The thrid he kepede clene for his drynke,	The third he kept untainted for himself,
prepared, labour	For al the night he schop him for to swynke	Meaning to toil at carrying his pelf
	In carying of the gold out of that place.	From out that cursed place the whole night long.
rioter	And whan this riotour, with sorry grace,	And when this villain, bent on doing wrong,
	Hath fillid with wyn his grete botels thre,	Had filled his three great bottles up with wine,
again	To his felaws ayein repaireth he.	Back to his mates he went, as if to dine.
sermonize	What nedith it therof to sermoun more?	What need is there of saying any more?
arranged	For right as they hadde cast † his deth bifore,	For as they had devised his death before,
have	Right so thay han him slayn, and that anoon.	E'en so they slew him, and with brief delay.

Vide the French—*outre mesure*, beyond measure. The common mediæval expressions, 'out of measure,' 'out of doubt,' were probably from the same word, *outre* = beyond.

* Tyrwhitt.

† Cast, as in '*cast* a nativity,' means fix upon, arrange, discover.

GLOSSARY.		
spake, one	And whan this was i-doon, thus spak that oon:	And when the deed was done, the first did say,
	Now let us drynke and sitte, and make us mery,	"Now let us sit and drink, and make us merry,
will	And afterwards * we wil his body bery.	And afterwards we will his body bury."
by chance	And with that word † it happed him *par cas*	And speaking thus, he chanced, upon the minute,
wherein	To take the botel ther the poysoun was,	To take a bottle which had poison in it,
gave	And drank, and yaf his felaw drink also,	And drank, and gave his fellow drink beside,
soon, died	For which anon thay stervede bothe two.	Whereby within a little space they died.
certainly	But certes I suppose that Avycen †	But truly I suppose that Avicen
wrote	Wrot never in *canoun*, ne in non *fen*,	Did ne'er describe in *canon* or in *fen*
wondrous pangs	Mo wonder sorwes of empoisonyng	More frightful pains of deadly poisoning,
	Than hadde these wrecches tuo or here endyng.	Than these two wretches felt in perishing.
be	Thus endid been these homicides tuo,	Thus ended both the wicked homicides,
also	And eek the fals empoysoner also.	And that false-hearted poisoner besides.

Notes by the Way.

During the 12th, 13th, and 14th centuries the passion for gambling had spread from the highest to the very lowest class of the population. The practice of men drinking and playing themselves bare in the taverns, where both vices were encouraged by the taverners, was common enough to provoke numberless censures and caricatures, so much so that it is a mercy Sir Wilfrid Lawson was spared the spectacle. The Pardoner's Tale is one of the list.

The taverns were the resort of all the refuse of the people: the taverners found it suited them to act as pawnbrokers, advancing money on the clothes and property of the ne'er-do-wells who lacked cash to stake or to pay; and provided other attractions whereby men were tempted to various vices, and robbed during their drunken sleep. The language of these young rascals of both sexes is graphically condemned by the Pardoner; and gluttony is pointed out as the root of all evil, for which Adam fell.

Hazard was the game with which our rioters strove to 'drive away the day.' Mr. Wright, speaking of the use of dice, tells us, "In its simpler form, that of the game of hazard, in which the chance of each player rested on the mere throw of the dice, it was the common game of the low frequenters of the taverns—that class which lived upon the vices of society, and which was hardly looked upon as belonging to society itself." Men staked all they possessed, to the very clothes on their backs, on one cast.

Chaucer tells us contemptuously how the King of Parthia sent a pair of golden dice to King Demetrius in scorn, knowing he was a player, to express that he held his glory and renown at no value, being liable to disappear at any moment.

The three rioters were probably young men who had ruined themselves by folly and licence, and whose besetting sin, surviving all it throve on, urged them to any and every crime for the sake of renewed gratification. Their end is beyond measure frightful. For why?—*The fiend found him in such living that he had leave to bring him to grief*, says the severe old moralist.

The extreme beauty of this poem, even in a technical sense alone, is such that I lament the necessity of abridging it.

* Tyrwhitt.

† Avicen, Ebn Sina, an Arabian physician of the 10th century. *Fen*, apparently an Arabic word, is the name given to the sections of Avicenna's great work on physic, entitled *Canun*.—*Tyrwhitt*.

MINOR POEMS.

Complaint of Chaucer to his Purse.

GLOSSARY.

no one else — To yow, my purse, and to noon other wight,
    Complayn I, for ye be my lady dere;
I am so sorry now that ye been lyght, *
if   For certes, but-yf ye make me heavy cheer
I were   Me were as leef be layde upon my bere,
    For whiche unto your mercy thus I crye—
be thou Beeth hevy ageyne, or elles mote I dye!

vouchsafe } Now voucheth sauf this day, or hyt be nyghte,
before
sound   That I of yow the blissful soune may here,
    Or se your colour lyke the sunne bryghte,
rival   That of yelownesse hadde never pere!
rudder Ye be my lyfe! ye be myn hertys stere!
    Quene of comfort and goode companye,
    Beth hevy ayeyne, or elles moote I die!

life's   Now, purse, that ben to me my lyves lyghte,
saviour And saveour as doun in this worlde here,
    Oute of this toune helpe me thurgh your myght,
since, } Syn that ye wole nat bene my tresorere, †
treasurer
nigh   For I am shave ‡ as nye as is a frere.
    But I pray unto youre courtesye,
    Bethe hevy ayeyn, or elles moote I dye!

To you, my purse, and to no other wight,
    Complain I, for you are my lady dear;
I am so sorry now that you are light,
    For truly if you make me heavy cheer
    I would as lief be laid upon my bier.
Therefore unto your mercy thus I cry—
Be heavy again, or else I needs must die!

I prithee grant this day, ere it be night,
    That I once more your merry voice may hear,
Or see your colour like the sunshine bright,
    Whereof the yellowness had never peer!
    You are my life, and you my heart shall steer;
Queen of all comfort and good company,
Be heavy again, or else I needs must die!

Now, purse, who are to me my life, my light,
    And chief deliverer in this world here,
Out of this city help me, by your might,
    If you no more will be my treasure dear,
    For I am shaved as close as any frere.
But I beseech you of your courtesy,
Be heavy again, or else I needs must die!

---

* A play on the word: light also meant fickle or untrue.

† Tyrwhitt has treasure; Morris has *tresorere*, treasurer. The former seems the most appropriate to a lady-love. A similar expression is found in 'Li Congiés Adan d'Aras' (MS. de la Vallière, No. 2736 Bibl. Imp.), 'De mon cuer serés tresoriere.'

‡ Bereft of money as a friar's tonsure is of hair.

Two Rondeaux.

Glossary.		
slay	Youre two eyn will sle me sodenly,	Your fair two eyes will slay me suddenly,
sustain	I may the beauté of them not sustene,	I know not how to bear their beauty's sheen,
goeth	So wendeth it thorow-out my herte kene.	It pierceth all my heart athrough so keen.

    And but your wordes will helen hastely   And if your words heal not full speedily
        My hertis wound, while that it is grene,   My heart's deep wound, while still the wound is green,
    Youre two eyn will sle me sodenly,   Your fair two eyes will slay me suddenly,
        I may the beauté of them not sustene,   I know not how to bear their beauty's sheen,
        So wendeth it thorow-out my herte kene.   It pierceth all my heart athrough so keen.

tell   Upon my trouth I say yow feithfully   Upon my faith I tell you faithfully
are   That ye ben of my liffe and deth the quene,   Both of my life and death you are the queen,
        For with my deth the trouth shal be i-sene   For in my dying shall the truth be seen.
    Youre two eynwill sle me sodenly,   Your fair two eyes will slay me suddenly,
        I may the beauté of them not sustene,   I know not how to bear their beauty's sheen
        So wendeth it thorow-out my herte kene.   It pierceth all my heart athrough so keen.

    Syn I, fro Love escaped, am so fat,   Since I escaped from love, I am so fat,
taken   I nere thinke to ben in his prison lene: *   No more I shall his captive be so lean:
since, free   Syn I am fre, I counte him not a bene.   Since I am free, I count him not a bean!

    He may answere and seye this and that: He may reply, and answer this and that:
I care not   I do no fors, I speak ryght as I mene: I care not, for I speak but as I mean:
    Syn I, fro Love escaped am so fat.   Since I escaped from love, I am so fat,
        I nere thinke to ben in his prison lene: No more I shall his captive be so lean:
        Syn I am fre, I counte him not a bene.   Since I am free, I count him not a bean!

struck, slate   Love hath my name i-strike out of his sclat,   My name—out of his slate Love striketh that.
books   And he is strike out of my bokes clene   And he is struck out of my books as clean
means   For evermo, there is none other mene.   For evermore, there is no way between!
    Syn I, fro Love escaped am so fat,   Since I escaped from love, I am so fat,
        I nere thinke to ben in his prison lene: No more I shall his captive be so lean:
        Syn I am fre, I counte him not a bene.   Since I am free, I count him not a bean!

---

* Bell's edition reads *tene*, taken.

Virelai.

Glossary		
	Alone walkyng,	Alone walk I,
mourning	In thought pleynyng	With many a sigh
	And sore syghyng,	In secrecy,
	Al desolate,	All desolate,
remembering	Me remembryng	And still review
my way of living	Of my lyvyng,	My life anew:
wishing	My deth wyshyng	For death I sue
	Bothe erly and late.	Both early and late.
unfortunate	Infortunate	My fate doth grow
so	Is soo my fate	So luckless now
	That, wote ye whate?	That—do you know?
beyond measure	Oute of mesure	Beyond all telling
	My lyfe I hate,	My life I hate:
	Thus, desperate,	Thus, desperate,
poor	In suche pore estate	In woeful state
remain	Do I endure.	I still am dwelling.
	Of other cure	I am not sure
not	Am I nat sure;	Of any cure;
	Thus to endure	'Tis hard t' endure
	Ys hard, certayn!	With no relief!
use	Suche ys my ure,	But certain 'tis,
assure	I yow ensure:	My state is this:
	What creature	What thing that is
	May have more payn?	Could have more grief?
truth	My trouth so pleyn	My story plain
taken	Ys take in veyn,	Is taken in vain,
	And gret disdeyn	With great disdain
remembrance	In remembraunce;	In recollection;
gladly	Yet I ful feyn	Yet I would fain
	Wolde me compleyn,	Alway complain,
to avoid	Me to absteyn	To shun the pain
penance	From thys penaunce.	Of this correction!

GLOSSARY.		
substance	But, in substaunce,	For which find I,
alleviation	None allegeaunce	Substantially,
grievance	Of my grevaunce	No remedy,
not	Can I nat fynd;	My lot to mend;
	Ryght so my chaunce	So fate, I see,
displeasure	With displesaunce	Still draws on me
advance	Doth me avaunce;	More enmity—
	And thus an end.	And there's an end!

Notes by the Way.

Chaucer's 'Complaint to his Purse' was written, according to Mr. Furnivall, in September, 1399, when Chaucer was in distress for money, and sent to Henry IV. as a broad hint,—which was at once attended to.

It is a very clever piece of versification, like the 'Good Counsel,' &c., each line rhyming with the corresponding line in the other verses. He addresses his hapless purse as though it were his lady-love, and comically entreats her mercy, when he sees her inclined to be 'light.'

Mr. Furnivall's ingenious suggestion, that Chaucer's penury may possibly be due to his having dabbled in alchemy (an empirical branch of chemistry), is borne out by the technical knowledge displayed in the Canon's Yeoman's Tale.

We may add here—to defend our great man's character—that alchemy was believed in by many men of exceptional mental power. Roger Bacon, discoverer of gunpowder and the magnifying glass, is perhaps the greatest name among them; and vain as seemed much of their toil with crucibles and furnaces, alembics and aludels, we owe a great deal to the first meritorious alchemists, who really paved the way to modern chemistry.

There is no reason to suppose Chaucer had any vice likely to affect his pocket; but alchemy was the scientific mania of the day, and high and low were ready to risk fortune and health in pursuit of the philosopher's stone, the elixir of life, the way to manufacture gold. And, at the same time, there is no other sufficient reason for the extreme poverty which the poet had fallen into.

The two Roundels and the Virelai have been asserted and denied to be the work of Chaucer, but there is no clear evidence for either side. They may well be a portion of those many lost 'ditties and songs glad' with which Gower said 'the land fulfilled is over all,' written 'in the floures of his youth.' The second Roundel seems, on the other hand, to belong to his later life, when he so often alluded to his corpulence. As to the Virelai, this species of lyric was nery fashionable in Chaucer's time. It is skilful work, each stanza rhyming six lines together (which I have failed to follow in the translation).

Good Counsel of Chaucer.

GLOSSARY.

mob, honesty	Fle fro the pres, and duelle with sothfastnesse,
thee, it	Suffice the thy good, though hit be smale,
hoards, uncertainty	For horde hath hate, and clymbyng tikelnesse,
deceived everywhere	Pres hath envye, and wele is blent over alle.
taste	Savour no more then the behove shalle;
	Rede * well thy self, that other folke canst rede,
without fear	And trouthe the shal delyver, hit ys no drede.
	Peyne the not eche croked to redresse,
	In trust of hire that turneth as a balle,†
great peace lies, meddling	Grete rest stant in lytel besynesse.
awl	Bewar also to spurne ayein an nalle,‡
crock	Stryve not as doth a croke § with a walle:
	Deme ‖ thyselfe that demest others dede,
	And trouthe the shal delyver, hit ys no drede.
	That the ys sent receyve in buxomnesse,
	The wrasteling of this world asketh a falle;
here	Her is no home, her is but wyldyrnesse.
beast	Forth, pilgrime!—forth, best, out of thy stalle!
	Loke up on hye, and thonke God of alle!
give up, desire	Weyve thy lust, and let thy goste the lede,
	And trouthe shal the delyver, hit ys no drede.

Fly from the crowd, and dwell with truthfulness
   Contented with thy good, though it be small;
Treasure breeds hate, and climbing dizziness,
   The world is envious, wealth beguiles us all.
   Care not for loftier things than to thee fall;
Counsel thyself, who counsel'st others' need,
And truth thee shall deliver, without dread.

Pain thee not all the crooked to redress,
   Trusting to her who turneth as a ball,
For little meddling wins much easiness.
   Beware lest thou do kick against an awl,
   Strive not as doth a clay pot with a wall:
Judge thou thyself, who judgest others' deed,
And truth thee shall deliver, without dread.

All that is given take with cheerfulness,
   To wrestle in this world is to ask a fall;
Here is no home, here is but wilderness.
   Forth, pilgrim, forth!—forth, beast, out of thy stall!
   Look up on high, and thank thy God for all!
Cast by ambition, let thy soul thee lead,
And truth thee shall deliver, without dread.

---

* Tyrwhitt's and Bell's editions. Morris has 'Do wel.'
† Fortune with her wheel.
‡ 'Kick against the pricks.'
§ For the clay pot is the weaker of the two.
‖ Tyrwhitt. Morris has *daunte* and *dauntest* (Fr., *dompter*), meaning control.

Notes by the Way.

We have Mr. F. J. Furnivall's authority, as well as internal evidence, for believing that this pathetic little poem expresses Chaucer's feelings at the time of his expulsion from the Customs offices, the beginning of his period of misfortunes, and was written immediately after the calamity. We seem to gather scattered hints of recent 'wrestlings' before the blow came—vain attempts to elevate, and purify, and carry out reforms, to make straight crooked paths. Lost labour—*pain thee not all the crooked to redress!*—trusting to fortune (money being requisite to reform): for those who value peace of mind should let sleeping dogs lie. We seem to catch the echoes of stormy times, of personal recrimination, envy, hatred, and malice, against a 'climbing' man, protected by Court favour for many prosperous years, but at length within the reach of foes when that protection waxed powerless. Chaucer may, like many another man, have made no enemies till he was high enough to stand in some one's light, prosperous enough to be dangerous; but his month of power in Parliament ruined him. It is pretty certain that some vote of his, while sitting for Kent, caused his dismissal from office. It was a case of win all or lose all, and he lost. To fight against such odds were as idle as undignified: surely, indeed, but courting worse injuries, 'kicking against an awl.' When the weak and the strong strive together, it is the weak who suffers. The criticism upon others, which had failed to do good, were now best turned philosophically upon himself. That which the fountain gave forth returns again to the fountain, as a poet 500 years later has said. It is impossible, in reading these melancholy and stately lines, not to feel that they ring true, and betray the half-sarcastic disappointment of a well-meaning man, the resignation of a religious man, and the faith in right-dealing bringing its own reward of a thoroughly honest man.

It is probable that the loss to Chaucer in a pecuniary sense was very severe; and the suddenness of the blow may account for much of his after poverty. ∗ The loss may have come at a time when he had debts which it would be very hard to pay out of a diminished income—debts which may have hampered his whole after-life. His appointment of a deputy to the office of Clerk of the King's Works, in 1391, and his subsequent resignation of the office, appear to me to hint at ill-health, as may his death a year after getting his lease for fifty-three years of the tenement in Westminster, where he died.

The last verse of this poem is the most remarkable of the three. Full of just contempt for his enemies'
aspersions, and of hearty trust in the power of truth to set things right, he rises suddenly into a
passion of aspiration. Trying to be content with adversity, he is angry with himself for
feeling it so deeply. To wrestle in this world is but courting an overthrow. But
this is not our Home, this is but a desert leading to a higher state.
Forth, pilgrim! gird up thy loins with fresh vigour to journey
on. Forth, pilgrim! *forth, beast, out of the stall* of narrow
hopes and interests! look higher, and thank thy God
for all. To cast by all the soul's lets and
hindrances—to be led by the higher
self—that is the pilgrim's
longing, and that is the
sublimest hope of
the human
heart.

∗ See 'Notes by the Way,' p. 103.

NOTES ON THE PICTURES.

I.—FRONTISPIECE.

THE costumes of the Knight, Squire, Prioress and Nun, Monk, Friar, Clerk (represented by Chaucer himself), Franklin, the Wife of Bath, the Summoner, and his friend the smart Pardoner, Mine Host and the boy, have been respectively studied from MSS. of the period. The attire of the Knight is open to criticism, for the amount of armour he wears is certainly more than he need wear on so peaceful an errand; but a portion of his well-used plate may be permitted him if only to distinguish the man of war from the numerous men of peace in the train.

The chain-mail, worn under the plate, would, I think, most probably have been retained by the Knight during his pilgrimage. The numerous miniatures of mailed knights journeying for no sinister purpose, appear to me to prove that it was very constantly worn. Unlike the mail which preceded it, the Asiatic kind which came into use in the twelfth century was comparatively light, being formed of slight rings interlaced, and not riveted upon leather. The hood of mail, which hangs on his shoulders, would have been no inconvenience at all. It joined the habergeon of mail, over which was his gipon, 'stained,' probably, by the rubbing of his mailed arms.

If, however, it be objected that the gipon was often an under garment (*vide* Meyrick, vol. ii. pp. 20 and 21), we may suppose him to have left a heavy hauberk of plate behind him in London 'till called for.'

Prioresses and nuns are often depicted in violet, in the contemporary MSS.; I therefore preferred that colour as more agreeable than black. Gloves such as the Nun's, were occasionally worn in the fourteenth century; the present example is taken from the effigy of William of Colchester, Abbot of Westminster, d. 1420. Gloves of fur, for winter wear, were common in the reign of Henry III.

The harness of the horses, bells and saddles, the Nun's chest, the Summoner's cake (probably ornamental gingerbread), and other details, have also been carefully studied from MSS. and tapestries of the time.

The boy's whip is taken from several fourteenth century and earlier drawings of horse-whips and whips for tops, and was therefore probably a common form.

The distant city is not necessarily London, as I failed to find a contemporary view of old London. The present sketch is borrowed from a fine MS. of Lydgate's poem, the 'Storie of Thebes' (MS. Reg. 18 D. ii.), and gives a good notion of the general look of a mediæval town.

Chaucer's portrait here was originally from the painting in the Harl. MS. 4866. I have no excuse to offer for changing the colour of Chaucer's gown from the grey or black in which Occleve always represented him to green, a very common colour at the time, except that it looked better in the picture, and we have no right to assume that Chaucer, even in his poorest days, had only one gown.

II.—DINNER IN THE OLDEN TIME.

The ordinary dinner-table or 'festive *board*' in a Franklin's or burgher's house has been taken from numerous fourteenth century illustrations. (*Vide* MS. Reg. 2 B. viii., and MS. Imp. Lib. Paris, No. 7210, &c.)

The carver, cupbearer, the fishbones left on the table in the absence of plates, the trenchers or slices of stale bread or buns used in lieu of them, and the other objects upon the table, are faithful copies from the MSS.

A minstrel was constantly employed to make music during the repast. The instrument here introduced is the cittern, played with or without a plectrum or quill. Behind are the servitors bringing in a pasty, some small birds on spits, and the nef or ship, containing salt, liqueurs, spices, or towel, &c., for washing the hands—or, if you like, it is a *sotelté* in the form of a ship. A subtlety was an ornamental dish that usually closed each course, made in some fanciful form, such as a castle, ship, or animal.

The dogs are munching the waste victuals under the table—such dogs being usually admitted during meals.

The pattern on the tablecloth is derived from a hunting-horn of the fourteenth century.

The peculiar folds at the sides of the tablecloth, which appear in many MSS., must, I think, have been purposely made for ornament, as we sometimes still see waiters crease cloths in various devices.

The sweet herbs strewn on the floor denote summer-time, in contradistinction to straw, which was used in the winter.

III.—LADY CROSSING STREET.

The background of shops and other buildings is borrowed mainly from the decapitation of G. de Pommiers at Bordeaux in 1377 (Froissart's Chronicle, No. 2644, Bibl. Imp. de Paris).

The costumes are those of middle-class persons. The clogs were in vogue with the long-toed boots.

Some of the streets were paved with large round stones, as in many French towns at the present day; others were not paved at all, and were, during wet weather, many feet deep with mud. An open channel or sewer ran along the midroad, which did not greatly add to the felicity of 'a walk down Fleet Street.'

IV.—FAIR EMELYE.

Emelye's garb is that common to the thirteenth and fourteenth centuries—a simple form with double sleeves. It will be remembered that Palamon mistook Emelye at first sight for a goddess; Arcite perceived her to be human. I have endeavoured to give the two men's views of her—each quite possible according to her position in the garden. Palamon may have caught sight of her just at a turn where the dazzle of sunrise behind the tree would be certain to lend a kind of halo to the outline of a head against it. An instant afterwards Emelye may have moved aside, the false halo disappearing, and she would seem what she truly was, simply an attractive maiden.

It is disappointing to find how very few were the flowers that adorned a mediæval garden. Our handsomest flowers were of course unknown—*e.g.*, the immense catalogue of plants introduced from America and elsewhere. Many that 'have had their day and ceased to be' in fashion, were as yet unknown too; such as the sunflower, which was imported about the sixteenth century. The red and white may, the dogrose, primrose, and the flowers that we banish to the kitchen garden or admire only in the fields, formed the chief ornaments. We find nettles and nightshade reckoned among garden plants; the dandelion, which appears in the place of honour in many old tapestries, was then counted as a flower.

The big round tower is one of the chain of fortresses linked by a solid wall running around the domain, from one of which the captive knights saw Emelye, her garden being within the walls, and, as the castle was generally built on an eminence, on higher ground than the flat country beyond.

Shining yellow in the sun-rise light is a conventional view of a city—the city of Athens, which Palamon and Arcite could see from their prison window.

V.—GRISELDA'S MARRIAGE.

The huts where poor persons lived were, of course, very rude, and lacked windows, doors, or chimneys. Orifices in the roof or sides served these purposes. The dirt from the smoke upon walls and ceiling was consequently considerable. The draught beasts dwelt with their owners, much as the Hibernian pig resides with Pat and his family.

The hairy hat surmounting the hood came into use during the fourteenth century, and was made of skins, dressed fur outward.

Griselda's raggedness must not be construed into slovenliness. Needles were not as accessible to the mass of the poor as they are now; and moreover, the poor not being then compulsorily educated, an honest, industrious girl who could work in the fields and spin, was not always able to darn.

VI.—GRISELDA'S BEREAVEMENT.

It is expressly stated that when her child was taken from her Griselda controlled her feelings, and did not so much as sigh. The sergeant finds her in her chamber, or bower, more private than the hall, and more luxuriously furnished. She is sitting in one of the high-backed chairs which usually stood near the bed's head (*vide* various fourteenth century MSS.)—possibly a *Prie-Dieu*—raised on a dais.

Her dress is simple, but that of the upper classes in Edward III.'s reign, lined with vair, and having long tippets from the sleeves knotted for convenience; her hair adorned with 'bends' or silken straps, and a gold head-dress. Her distaff is still at hand, and the full basket betokens her continued industry. Floor-carpets or mats, embroidered or woven, were rare at this time, and could only have been in use in a wealthy house; but they are occasionally spoken of in early MSS. In 'Gautier d'Aupais' an old lady is described as sitting on a richly-worked counterpoint, by a coal fire; but this may have been a cloth flung over a chair; and in the romance of 'Queen Berthe' three persons are said to sit on carpets (*sur les tapis*).

It will be remembered that the dagger was frequently used with the left hand.

VII.—DORIGEN AND AURELIUS.

The parti-coloured dress worn by Aurelius, similar to the Squire's in the frontispiece, was common in Edward III.'s reign, and was peculiarly obnoxious to the satirists of the day. The cote-hardie or close-fitting tunic sometimes matched in colour one of the legs, sometimes was divided into halves of opposing colours; the shoes were very rich and of contrary hues also.

The ladies' gowns were long and of very rich materials, the arms bound with gold, and further adorned by fantastic streamers or tippets. Chess was the fashionable pastime of old and young. The pieces in this picture are from some ivory Icelandic chessmen of the twelfth century.

Behind is the lawn where Dorigen's *meinie*, or pages and household attendants, are amusing themselves with dancing and ball-playing among the enclosed flower-beds peculiar to the mediæval pleasure-garden.

The coat of arms repeated upon Aurelius' dress is that attributed to Chaucer. The instrument, on which he doubtless accompanied his mournful love-songs, is a form of cittern. The carved design upon the settle or seat is Anglo-Saxon; the *fleur de lys* on the curtain of the tent beside them was a common ornament.

I have not been able to discover at what precise date 'shot' materials came into use. There are many singular terms applied to the colours of dress throughout the middle ages, such as *pourpre-gris*, *ecarlate-blanche*, &c. In the 'Fabliau de Gautier d'Aupais' there is mention of '*un vert mantel porprine*' (a mantle of green crimson). In my own mind I am persuaded that these terms, explicable easily in no other way, refer to shot materials. Mediæval miniatures and pictures also bear out this theory, dresses being depicted of certain colours shaded with certain others in strong contrast. The commonest is blue or red shaded with gold. There have been many conjectures with regard to the above terms. M. le Grand supposes that rare dyes, being chiefly used to dye rich cloths, gave at last their names to those cloths, irrespective of colour. The *Saturday Review* once accused the old masters of "sporting with pigments prismatically" when they used red as the shadow of green, &c., oblivious of the fact that if the early masters had a fault it was adhering too blindly to nature in their works. It is clear that in Quentin Matsys' day (fifteenth century) shot materials were quite common, for there is scarcely one of his pictures without a study of the kind. In his 'Dead Christ' at Antwerp several unmistakable examples occur; in his 'Virgin' at Amsterdam is introduced a curtain of green and brown shot. This being so, we have no reasonable ground for believing that shot silks, though not yet common, were unknown a century earlier.

I have therefore given two marked examples of similar silks, in the robes of Griselda and Dorigen, both wealthy enough to import such fabrics if in existence at all.

VIII.—THE RIOTER.

The ordinary cheap wine used in the middle ages was often carried in 'bottles' or pitchers of this form.

A longish gown was the dress of the commoner people in the fourteenth century. The Rioter is intended to represent a man of decent position, but not noble, who has come to the end of his tether, in a pecuniary sense, and whose slovenly hose and young but debauched and cruel face indicate with what facility he has been degraded by his elder companions.

PORTRAIT OF CHAUCER.

Chaucer's portrait is copied from a drawing by Occleve the poet (Brit. Mus. Harl. MS. 4866). Occleve made, or caused to be made, shortly after Chaucer's death, several portraits of him, of which two remain; and on these are founded the many now scattered over the country. The same features recur in all. The peculiar aquiline nose, mouth a little drooping, eyes downcast, the forked beard and fair complexion, the broad round jaw, are the same in all. Occleve always depicted Chaucer with a rosary in his hand, and his penner, containing his pen and inkhorn, hanging to his vest. His hands are small and well-shapen, his form is portly, his air calm, benevolent, almost pathetic.

These lines run beside the miniature in Occleve's MS.:—

Glossary.		
extinguished	Al thogh his lyfe be queynt, the resemblaunce	Although his life be quench'd, so clear doth lie
liveliness	Of him hath in me so fressh lyflynesse	Within my mind the living look of him,
	That to putte othir men in remembraunce	That to put other men in memory
likeness	Of his persone I have heere his lyknesse	Of his appearance, here his face I limn,
had made (*faire faire*), truth	Do make, to this end in sothfastnesse,	That they to whom his image groweth dim,
lost	That thei that have of him lest thought and mynde	And they that have of him lost thought and mind,
painting	By this peynture may ageyn him fynde.	By this poor portrait may again him find.

The portraits by Occleve, his personal friend and disciple, whose deep affection for Chaucer is touchingly reiterated in his 'Lament' for him, may be relied on as most conscientious pictures from memory of the great poet's habitual appearance.

Notes on the Woodcuts.

THE TOURNAMENT. (See Title-page.)—There must always have been, to some extent, a grotesque element in the Tournament. The desire to be conspicuous forced the combatants to assume the gayest and the biggest decoration. At a later date the tilting helmets sprouted into the most preposterous sizes and shapes. Figures and 'favours' assumed for the occasion, the gifts of enthusiastic lady-loves, as well as hereditary devices, surmounted the helm and glittered on coat-armour and harness. In Edward III.'s reign the beauty and *éclat* of the tourney was in its zenith; in Richard II.'s the beautiful began to be overpowered by the grotesque. I have tried to tone down the grotesque as much as may be, but a general dazzle and confusion of colour is inseparable from the scene, vivid, violent, and exciting as it was. Tents were often erected within the pale of the lists for the convenience of those awaiting or *hors de combat*. Shields or targets, for *peace* or *war*, were suspended in couples before them, emblazoned with the arms of each lord; and whoso sent to touch the targets was tilted with according to his wish—*i.e.*, with sharp or blunt lances.

The end of Theseus' tourney was clearly a riot, but I have preferred to represent the orderly onset of the first combatants, guided by a MS. Froissart of the fifteenth century. It has been suggested to me that it would be impossible to tilt across the bar unless the spear-arm were next the bar, as the horse's neck would impede the stroke, and the rider's own spear would unhorse him: in tent-pegging and all sports with the lance the rider brings his spear-arm next the mark. But having found several early miniatures in which the spear is aimed as here given, I considered myself justified in trusting to contemporary MSS. in spite of modern theories.

The horses were the chief sufferers in these mimic frays. The heavy beasts, protected as they were by a great weight of armour, were often injured. The best-trained dreaded the shock of encounter, and, as we read in Froissart, their restiveness and swerving at the last moment frequently spoiled the 'course,' despite the most violent spurring, to their masters' deep chagrin and disappointment, and the disgust of the lady-loves.

The high saddles, sometimes locking the rider in his seat all round, were constructed to retain him on his horse, however violent the push; but they were the cause of many an unhappy accident. Death like Arcite's, from crushing against the saddle-bow, was by no means uncommon. So died William the Conqueror himself four hundred years before; when, riding down the steep street of Mantes, his horse stumbled among the embers he had kindled. (See Green's Short History of the English People, p. 85.)

Suffocation in the dust was a still more frequent cause of death; as thrown riders could not rise, nor rid themselves of their ponderous casques.

Skill rather than strength was needful in tilting. The spear, as in pig-sticking in India, was thrust rather by the weight of the horse than by the weight of the arm. Strength of back and arm were necessary to avoid being bent backwards or driven over the crupper; but extreme skill was requisite to hit one's slippery foe with anything like force. When both knights hit their mark so that fire flew from their helmets, without either falling, it was reckoned a 'handsome course.'

A word about the allans, as big as bullocks, which went leaping around Lycurgus' car. They were undoubtedly a kind of mastiff, large and powerful; they wore gold collars filled with *torettz*. This word is variously explained. *Torete*, ring-turret (Morris), ring or terret (Bell). '*Toret*, a small wimble (or auger, big gimblet). Touret, a drill, &c.' (Cotgrave). '*Gros clou dont la tête arrondie est arrêtée dans une branche d'un mors*' (Suppl. to Fr. Acad. Dict.).

I have ventured on translating 'toret' *spike*, after vainly seeking for authority for a collar filled with rings; though a single ring often hung beneath the throat. Contemporary illustrations of dogs' collars filled with long spikes are common enough—*e.g.* the fine fourteenth century tapestry now in the museum at Chartres, &c.

In India dogs are furnished with spiked collars in tiger and boar hunting: the allans were clearly hunting dogs, and such spiked collars would thus be almost indispensable.

JOHN OF GAUNT, Royal Coll. 20 B. 6. (See page 7.)—This portrait has an air of truth about it; in the MS. it is very carefully and delicately worked. The gown is of a reddish murrey colour, with ermine or miniver lining to skirt and sleeves, the under sleeves being blue. His hose are red, and he wears a golden circlet, necklace, and belt. One can trace some resemblance to Edward III., his father, in the long, narrow, but not unpleasing face. Other portraits of John of Gaunt have the same features. The hair and beard are grey. He appears to be respectfully lecturing the young King Richard, who is seated on his throne, receiving a book presented by a monk, in the presence of his three royal uncles.

SHIP. (See page 8.)—How such ships could sail is a mystery, but this is the most usual anatomy for a man-of-war, or for a 'subtlety' at dinner in the form of a ship. I copied the present example from a MS. in the British Museum: it is one of a royal fleet. There is a Nef introduced in the famous 'Nancy' tapestry (fifteenth century) of precisely the same construction.

STYLUS. (See page 10.)—The stylus was used for writing on waxen tablets. No doubt wax was cheaper and more easily procured than parchment or paper; paper made from rags being then quite a recent invention, and probably what was made was not white but brown, and imported from abroad. Wax could be dissolved and used again. Hence we find, in the romance of 'Flor and Blanchflor,' the king putting children to school, where they learned to write

Letres et vers d'amors en cire,	Letters and verses of love on the wax.
Lor greffes sont d'or et d'argent.	Their styles are of gold and silver.

THE YEOMAN. (See page 21.)—The term 'not-head' used by Chaucer may mean that he had his hair closely cropped—a head like a nut—as suggested by Tyrwhitt, &c.; but I think, on the contrary, it refers to his hood having the liripipe knotted around it, as there are numerous instances of such hoods worn by foresters, hunters, and others, to whom a long tail would be a nuisance, if not actually dangerous. The woodcut of a knotted hood, on p. 2, is that of a forester, in the Book of Gaston Phœbus, fourteenth century, in the National Library of Paris. Chaucer says the miller wore his 'typet ybounde about his heed' ('Reeve's Tale,' line 33).

THE PRIORESS. (See page 22.)—Her costume (same as in Frontispiece) is borrowed from an Abbess or Prioress in a MS. of the History of the Emperors (Lib. of the Arsenal), fifteenth century.

THE MONK. (See page 24.)—From Royal MS. 14 E. 4, temp. Ed. IV.: too late, indeed, but it appears that the clerical costume had suffered no great change.

THE CLERK. (See page 27.)—The figure of the Clerk possesses peculiar interest, as it represents one of those ancient artists whose paintings in mediæval MSS. are so valuable to us now. His name is Alan Strayler, a designer and painter, and his dress is that of an ordinary middle-class man; it will be seen to be precisely similar to Chaucer's, who was himself a 'clerk.'

THE SERJEANT AT LAW. (See page 28.)—It is curious that the mantle of this figure, whose dress is taken from two effigies of Chief Justices of the King's Bench in the fourteenth century, should recall the Roman toga, being apparently fastened over the hood, on the right shoulder, so as to leave that arm completely free: an instance of the conservatism of official dress, which alters very little with the fluctuations of fashion, whilst those persons whose costume denotes no position are constantly undergoing protean changes.

THE DOCTOR. (See page 29.)—The medical man is as much too early as the monk is too late, but it was the most characteristic one I could find, and I preferred thirteenth century to fifteenth century costume. The mantle recalls the Roman toga. (Copy from Sloane Coll. No. 1975.)

THE PARSON. (See page 30.)—See a brass of John Islyngton, vicar of Islington, in Norfolk, in 1393. The dress of a plain parish priest is not often represented: it will be seen to be not dissimilar to that of a modern French priest.

THE PLOUGHMAN.—(See page 31.)—Studied from figures in a very ancient Anglo-Saxon MS. It appears to me that the liripipe (evidently then worn) is in this case twisted around the head.

THE PARDONER. (See page 31.)—The Pardoner may have worn the ordinary clerkly gown, or, as in the Frontispiece, a close-fitting garb. Chaucer does not describe his attire, but says he thought himself 'al of the newe get' (*i.e.*, fashion).

PRINCIPAL AUTHORITIES CONSULTED IN THIS BOOK.

Sir S. Meyrick, 'Antient Armour.'

Lacroix, 'Manners, Customs, and Dress during the Middle Ages,' &c., &c.

Skeat, 'Chaucer,' &c.

Morris, 'Chaucer' (Aldine edition), 1866, and 'Chaucer' (Clarendon Press), 1874.

Tyrwhitt's 'Chaucer.'

Bell's edition of 'Chaucer's Poetical Works.'

Fairholt, 'Costume in England.'

Wright, 'Domestic Manners during the Middle Ages,' and 'Womankind in Western Europe.'

Froissart's 'Chronicles.'

Planché, 'British Costume.'

Shaw, 'Dresses and Decorations,' 'Ornaments,' &c.

Furnivall, 'Babee's Book,' and 'Trial Forewords' (Chaucer Society), &c.

'Arthur of Britayn.'

Six-Text Edition of Chaucer's 'Canterbury Tales.'

Bonnard & Mercurj, 'Costumes des XIIIe, XIVe, et XVe Siècles,' 1840.

Le Grand, 'Fabliaux et Contes du XIIe et du XIIIe Siècle,' 1781.

Barbazan, 'Fabliaux et Contes,' 1808.